ENGLISH

Gillian Howell
Series Editor: **Richard Cooper**

RISING STARS

PLEASE NOTE: THIS BOOK MAY NOT BE PHOTOCOPIED OR REPRODUCED AND WE APPRECIATE YOUR HELP IN PROTECTING OUR COPYRIGHT.

Rising Stars UK Ltd., 22 Grafton Street, London W1S 4EX

www.risingstars-uk.com

All facts are correct at time of going to press.

First published 2003
This edition 2008
Reprinted 2009, 2010

Text, design and layout © Rising Stars UK Ltd.

First edition written by: Gill Matthews, Alison Clarke, Laura Collins and Richard Cooper
Educational consultant: Emily Nutt
Project management: Cambridge Publishing Management Ltd.
Project editor: Tom Willsher
Illustrations: Phill Burrows and Clive Wakfer
Design: Neil Adcock
Cover design: Burville-Riley Partnership

Acknowledgements
pp52–53 from *Smile!* by Geraldine McCaughrean (OUP, 2004) © Geraldine McCaughrean 2004. Published and used with the permission of Oxford University Press; p56 from *Alone on a Wide Wide Sea* by Michael Morpurgo (HarperCollins Children's Books, 2006); p58 Ian McMillan 'Ten things found in a wizard's pocket' and 'Counting the stars' © 2001 from *The Very Best of Ian McMillan* © Ian McMillan. Published and used with the permission of Macmillan Children's Books.

British Library Cataloguing in Publication Data
A CIP record for this book is available from the British Library.

ISBN 978-1-84680-284-3

Printed by Craft Print International Ltd, Singapore

Contents

How to use this book

Writing non-fiction

1 **Definition** – This describes the genre and provides examples of the text type.

2 **Text type** – Each type of writing is explained in a step-by-step way to help you plan.

3 **Self-assessment** – Tick the face that best describes your understanding of this concept.

4 **Text plan** – Planning is very important when writing fiction and non-fiction, and these charts will help you to plan properly. You are given planning time in the tests, so make sure you use it!

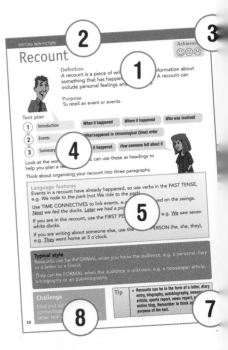

5 **Language features** – This explains the language features used for this type of text, including examples.

6 **Text example** – This gives you an example of a well-written piece of text that follows the text plan and contains key language features.

7 **Tips** – Here you are given key hints and tips to help you achieve Level 4.

8 **Challenge** – Here you are asked to find features contained in the text example. The answers can be found on pages 62–64.

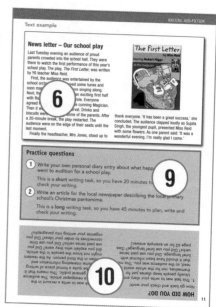

9 **Practice questions** – This is where you do the work! Try answering the questions by using the text plan and by referring to the key language features. Compare your work with the written example – is it good enough for Level 4?

10 **How did you do?** – Read the questions – can you answer 'yes' to each of them?

Writing fiction

This section takes you through the key elements of writing fiction:

1 **Structure** – This section provides a model structure for your fiction writing including examples.

2 **Setting, character and theme** – This section explains the key ingredients for writing fiction and explores each ingredient in depth.

3 **Planning** – This section provides you with a structure to use before you begin writing a story.

4 **Challenge** – The challenges ask you to find features contained in the text example.

5 **Tips** – The tips give you ideas and hints to improve your work and get the best marks.

Reading comprehension

1 **Text examples** – These give you typical examples of a piece of text that you might find in your National Tests.

2 **Tips** – These give you suggestions on how to read the text and questions to ask yourself while reading.

3 **Questions** – The text is followed by a number of questions relating to the text. There are 1-, 2- and 3-mark questions, so remember to read between the lines.

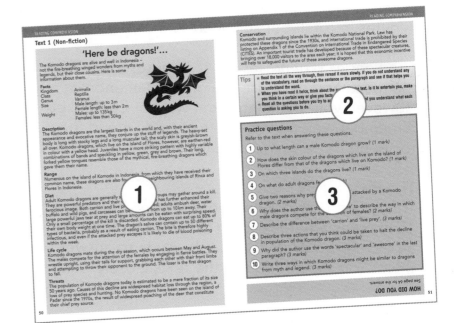

In addition you will find over 100 clear tips and facts to help you with:
grammar   spelling   punctuation   vocabulary   handwriting

A glossary of terms can be found on page 60.

If you use this guidance to help you prepare for your test you will have a great chance of achieving Level 4!

About the National Tests

Key facts

- The Key Stage 2 National Tests take place in the summer term in Year 6. You will be tested on Maths and English.

- The tests take place in your school and will be marked by examiners – not your teacher!

- Individual scores are not made public. However, a school's combined scores are published in what are commonly known as 'league tables'.

The English National Tests

You will take four tests in English. These are designed to test your reading, writing and spelling. Your handwriting will be assessed through the Longer Writing Task.

The Writing Tasks

There are two Writing Tasks – one shorter and one longer task. Remember to keep your handwriting neat for these tasks.

The *Shorter Writing Task* is 20 minutes long. You should plan very briefly using the given prompts in no longer than two to three minutes. Remember that you only have 20 minutes in total, but still need to include a one-minute check at the end.

The *Longer Writing Task* is 45 minutes long. You should aim for 10 minutes' planning at the most. You must use the given plan and not any other separate paper or planner. However, your planning sheet will not be marked so you do not need to be neat. But remember, you must be able to understand the notes on your plan! Remember ALWAYS to spend three to five minutes at the end for rereading and checking.

The Reading Test

This is one test to assess your reading comprehension. It will last one hour; the first 15 minutes are for reading the texts. In this test you will be given a series of texts and an answer booklet. You use the texts to answer the questions so you need not memorise them. You should refer to the texts closely while you are answering.

The Spelling Test

The spelling test is 10 minutes long. Your test paper will have the text of a passage with some words missing. Your teacher will read the complete passage (or play a CD of someone else reading it). You will then hear the passage a second time, during which you have to write the missing words in the spaces on your test paper.

Test techniques

Before the test

(1) When you revise, try revising 'little and often' rather than in long sessions.

(2) Read the hints and tips throughout the book to remind you of important points.

(3) Revise with a friend. You can encourage and learn from each other.

(4) Be prepared – bring your own pens and pencils.

During the test

(1) READ THE QUESTION, THEN READ IT AGAIN.

(2) If you get stuck, don't linger on the same question – move on! You can come back to it later.

(3) Never leave a multiple-choice question. Make an educated guess if you really can't work out the answer.

(4) Check to see how many marks a question is worth. Have you 'earned' those marks with your answer?

(5) Check your answers after each question. Does your answer look correct?

Where to go to get help

Pages 9, 20, 32 and 49 provide you with a description of what you should aim to do when you are reading and writing at Level 4. You can refer to them at any time to check you are keeping on track to achieve Level 4!

Pages 8–31 are designed to help you succeed in the Writing Test and include information about writing fiction and non-fiction.

Pages 32–43 will help you give 'voice' to your writing, sharpen up your punctuation and improve your grammar.

Pages 44–46 give you practice in spelling, including a list of key words to learn before your test.

Pages 48–58 are designed to help you succeed in the Reading Test and include reading fiction, non-fiction and poetry.

Page 60 contains a glossary to help you understand key terms about writing, reading and grammar.

Pages 62–64 provide the answers to the practice questions.

Writing non-fiction

Achieved?

🙂 😐 ☹

Non-fiction texts give you information about something or someone.
They also give you facts and, sometimes, opinions.

Type of non-fiction	Definition and purpose	Where you might read an example
Recount	Tells you about something that has already happened. It may include personal opinions and comments	Letters, diaries, newspapers, biographies, autobiographies, magazines
Instructions and procedures	Tell you how to do something in a step-by-step way	Board game instructions, recipes, directions, how to make or repair something
Non-chronological report	Gives you facts about a topic or subject	Encyclopaedias, information books, posters, leaflets, travel guides
Explanation	Tells you how or why something happens or works	Leaflets, posters, manuals, letters, diagrams, information books
Discussion	Gives you information both for and against a topic	Newspaper articles, letters, magazines, information leaflets, posters, speeches
Persuasion	Tries to influence how you think about someone or something	Advertisements, articles, leaflets, spam emails, letters

Tips	
	★ The tasks in the non-fiction Writing Test do not always tell you what text type you need to write. They often just say *'Write an information text ...'* ★ So it is important that you: • think carefully about the *purpose* and *audience* you are writing for. This will help you know what type of text to write • use the correct structure and language features • organise your writing into paragraphs • use connectives thoughtfully • vary the length and type of your sentences • try to be adventurous with your choice of words

Achieve Level 4 writing

At Level 4 your writing is lively and thoughtful. You can develop your ideas and organise them according to the purpose of your writing. You can make adventurous choices of vocabulary and use words for effect. You can use complex sentences, and your spelling and punctuation is usually accurate. Your handwriting is fluent, joined and legible.

Over to you!

- Work through each section and don't rush.
- Learn the purpose of the text type.
- Make sure you understand the way it is organised and the key language features.
- Have a go at the challenges and the practice questions.

Tips	The practice questions
	★ Decide what the *purpose* of the writing is. This is the clue to which text type to write. E.g. *Write a letter describing a weekend away …* Straight away this tells you the text should be a RECOUNT. *Write a letter to persuade someone to …* Straight away this tells you to write a PERSUASIVE text. Get the idea?	★ Decide who the *audience* is. This is the clue to what sort of language to include. E.g. *Write a letter to your best friend …* This tells you to use informal language because you know the audience well. *Write a report for the local museum on …* This tells you to use polite, formal language because you don't know exactly who will be reading it. Get the idea?

ALWAYS READ THE QUESTION AT LEAST TWICE!

Once you have decided on the purpose and audience, plan, write and check your writing.

Recount

Definition
A recount is a piece of writing that gives information about something that has happened in the past. A recount can include personal feelings and comments.

Purpose
To retell an event or events.

Text plan

1 Introduction   ***When* it happened**   ***Where* it happened**   ***Who* was involved**

2 Events   ***What* happened in chronological (time) order**

3 Summary   ***Why* it happened**   ***How* someone felt about it**

Look at the words in *italics*. You can use these as headings to help you plan a recount.

Think about organising your recount into three paragraphs.

Language features
Events in a recount have already happened, so use verbs in the PAST TENSE, e.g. *We rode to the park* (not *We ride to the park*).

Use TIME CONNECTIVES to link events, e.g. <u>First</u> *we played on the swings.* <u>Next</u> *we fed the ducks.* <u>Later</u> *we had a picnic.*

If you are in the recount, use the FIRST PERSON (*I, we, us*), e.g. <u>We</u> *saw seven white ducks.*

If you are writing about someone else, use the THIRD PERSON (*he, she, they*), e.g. <u>They</u> *went home at 5 o'clock.*

Typical style
Recounts can be INFORMAL when you know the audience, e.g. a personal diary or a letter to a friend.

They can be FORMAL when the audience is unknown, e.g. a newspaper article, a biography or an autobiography.

Challenge
Find and list the time connectives in the News letter text example (page 11).

Tip   ★ Recounts can be in the form of a letter, diary entry, biography, autobiography, newspaper article, sports report, news report, email or online blog. Remember to think about the purpose of the text.

Text example

News letter – Our school play

(Last) Tuesday evening an audience of proud parents crowded into the school hall. They were there to watch the first performance of this year's school play. The play, *The (First) Letter*, was written by Y6 teacher Miss Reid.

(First) the audience was entertained by the school orchestra. They played some tunes and soon many of the parents were singing along. (Next,) the play started. It was an exciting first half with Robert Higgs in the lead role. Everyone agreed he was fantastic as the cunning Magician. Then it was time for the interval. Drinks and biscuits were served by some of the parents. After a 20-minute break, the play restarted. The audience were on the edge of their seats until the (last) moment.

(Finally) the headteacher, Mrs Jones, stood up to

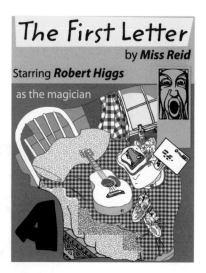

The First Letter
by *Miss Reid*
Starring **Robert Higgs**
as the magician

thank everyone. 'It has been a great success,' she concluded. The audience clapped loudly as Sujata Singh, the youngest pupil, presented Miss Reid with some flowers. As one parent said: 'It was a wonderful evening. I'm really glad I came.'

Practice questions   X

1 Write your own personal diary entry about what happened when you went to audition for a school play.

This is a **short** writing task, so you have 20 minutes to plan, write and check your writing.

2 Write an article for the local newspaper describing the local primary school's Christmas pantomime.

This is a **long** writing task, so you have 45 minutes to plan, write and check your writing.

HOW DID YOU DO?

Now go back and check your work!

1. This task was to write your diary entry. Usually people keep diaries just for themselves, not for the whole world to read, so the audience was you. This means that it should have been informal with brief language. Did you use past tense verbs? Did you use brief language? (See page 62 for an example answer.)

2. This task was to write a recount in the form of a newspaper article. The audience was the general public. This means that it should be quite a formal piece of writing with some interesting information and written in the third person. As the readers might not know the people in the article, did you explain who they were? Did you use past tense verbs? Did you use time connectives to order your ideas? Did you organise your writing into paragraphs?

Instructions and procedures

Achieved? ☺ ☹ ☹

Definition
Instructions tell the reader how to do, make or play something or how to get somewhere.

Purpose
To instruct.

Text plan

1. Aim

   This is the title and tells the reader what the instructions are about.

2. What you need

   A list of the things that are needed to achieve the aim. These are listed in order of use.

3. What you do

   A step-by-stepchronological (time order) sequence of what to do achieve the aim.

So, usually in instructions there is a title and two headings.

You need to decide on the best headings for the instructions you are writing.

A recipe could have *ingredients* and *method* as the headings.

Language features
Use amounts and quantities in the list of things that are needed, e.g.

3 counters   1 dice   1 pack of cards

You must write in the PRESENT TENSE. If you start to slip into the past tense, you are writing a recount!

Use commands or the IMPERITAVE VOICE. Put the verb at the beginning of the sentence, e.g. *Cut the paper into a circle.*

Write in the SECOND PERSON. Instructions are talking directly to the reader but you don't need to use the word 'you', e.g. 'Cut the paper.' not '<u>You</u> cut the paper.

Use CONNECTIVES that are time related e.g. *first, secondly, finally.*

Sometimes you might need to tell the reader how to carry out the instruction by using adverbs, e.g. <u>Carefully</u> *cut the paper.* The adverb can go before the verb at the beginning of the sentence.

You can use bullet points to help the reader.

Typical style
Use BRIEF LANGUAGE. The reader doesn't want lots of words to wade through if they are following instructions. Be careful not to overload sentences with detail.

| Tip | ★ Think 'step-by-step'. This will help you to order your writing. |

Text example

How to look after a pet dinosaur

What you need

A large garden or open space

Plenty of trees and shrubs

Fresh water

Sturdy container, e.g. bath

Scale polish

Lead

1 Your dinosaur needs plenty of room to roam. Allow him time to explore his new home. Keep an eye on him from a distance.

2 Feed your dinosaur on a regular basis by giving him plenty of fresh leaves and other greenery. Offer several litres of fresh water each day in a container that cannot easily be knocked over.

3 Gently clean the dinosaur with scale polish about twice a week. His skin should look supple.

4 Carefully place a lead around his neck in order to take him out in public. Teach him to follow you and to come when you call.

5 Take care of him and you will have a happy life with your pet dinosaur.

Practice questions

1 You know where there is some buried treasure on a small island in the middle of an ocean. A brave explorer has offered to go and get the treasure for you. Write some instructions that tell him where to find it.

This is a **long** writing task, so you have 45 minutes to plan, write and check your writing.

2 The aliens have landed and want to come to school! Write a set of instructions telling the aliens how to get dressed for school so that they will blend in with the rest of the pupils.

This is a **short** writing task, so you have 20 minutes to plan, write and check your writing.

HOW DID YOU DO?

Now go back and check your work!

1. This task was to write a set of instructions in the form of directions. The audience was a brave explorer looking for some buried treasure. This means that he would need detailed information about how to get to the treasure. You could have told him what landmarks to look out for on the route. Did you think about what he would need to take with him? You could have listed things like a rope and a spade.

2. This task was to write a set of instructions for getting dressed for school. The audience was a group of aliens. They would not be familiar with the names of human clothing nor how to put it on. You would need to describe clothes very carefully and give detailed instructions about how to put the clothes on. But, you only had 20 minutes. You didn't have time to get carried away! (See page 62 for an example answer.)

Non-chronological report

Achieved?

Definition
Non-chronological reports give a reader information about something or somewhere. They are usually about a group of things, e.g. *dinosaurs*, not one thing in particular, e.g. *Dilly the dinosaur*. Facts about the subject are organised into paragraphs.

Purpose
To give information.

Text plan

1 Title — Usually the subject of the report.

2 Introduction — Definition of the subject.

3 Series of paragraphs about various aspects of the subject — Facts usually grouped by topic.

4 Summary or rounding-off statement — Could be an unusual fact about the subject.

Paragraphs are the key to writing non-chronological reports. Try to use at least two paragraphs after the introduction and before the rounding-off statement.

Decide what each paragraph is going to be about and only have that information in there.

Language features
Use the PRESENT TENSE if the subject still exists, e.g. *Crocoraffes have, are, live.* Use the PAST TENSE if the subject is from the past, e.g. *Dinosaurs were, had, lived.*

Use TECHNICAL VOCABULARY (language about the subject), e.g. *Many dinosaurs were herbivores.*

Use FACTUAL ADJECTIVES to give more information about a fact, e.g. *They had very sharp teeth and strong jaws.*

Challenge
Write a key word to summarise each of the paragraphs in the text example on page 13.

Typical style
Use IMPERSONAL sentence starts, e.g. sentences that begin with *The crocoraffes ..., They are ..., It is ..., Crocoraffes ...*

Sentences that begin with *I, she, he, we* are personal sentence starts.

Remember always to use IMPERSONAL sentences.

Tip ★ Reports can be in the form of letters, encyclopaedia entries, information posters or leaflets, as well as straightforward pieces of writing.

Text example

Crocoraffes

Crocoraffes are large animals. They can breathe and eat, both in and out of water. They were discovered on 1 April 2008 by the explorer Sir Humbert Bumbert while he was trekking through dense jungle.

Crocoraffes are about the size of a large horse and have scaly skin that has a mottled effect. They have long necks, which they use to reach up into the highest branches for leaves. They also have very sharp teeth and strong jaws in order to catch their prey when swimming under water. The animal's broad muscular legs push it quickly through water.

Crocoraffes are omnivores. This means that they eat both leaves and meat. They are attracted by the tender new shoots of the honey tree and can cause considerable damage to these trees. In the water, crocoraffes will catch and eat up to fifty large fish in a day.

The jungles of South America appear to be the only place where crocoraffes can be found. They keep to the thickest part of the jungle that is rarely, if ever, visited by people. They make large nests from jungle creepers and line them with mud from the river bank. This hardens to create a sturdy home for a pair of crocoraffes and their offspring.

They can live for as long as forty to fifty years and mate for life. During this partnership a couple can produce as many as a hundred offspring, known as crocoraffettes.

Practice questions

Your task is to write a leaflet to display outside the main enclosure of Sir Humbert Bumbert's Butterfly Farm that houses all the rare and unusual butterfly species he has collected on his travels.

This is a **long** writing task, so you have 45 minutes to plan, write and check your writing.

The fossilised skeleton of a newly discovered type of dinosaur has been found. Your task is to write a poster to display in a children's museum to tell visitors about this type of dinosaur.

This is a **short** writing task, so you have 20 minutes to plan, write and check your writing.

HOW DID YOU DO?

Now go back and check your work!

1. The task was to write a report in the form of a leaflet. The leaflet will be displayed at the Butterfly Farm, so the audience would be the general public. This means that you needed to write in a formal style. In the introduction you should have briefly described what a butterfly farm is and what you can see there. In the next two or three paragraphs you should have chosen different things to write about in more detail, e.g. types of butterfly, habitat, life-cycle. Did you use present tense verbs? You should not have included very much about

2. Your task was to write a report in the form of a poster. This will be displayed at a children's museum so the audience is the general public, but as it is mainly for young people you could have used a slightly informal style. Did you still have the information organised into paragraphs? As this report was in the form of a poster, you should have used brief language. Did you use, for example, bullet points, tables or charts? (See page 62 for an example answer.)

how and where they were found or it will turn into a recount before your very eyes!

15

Explanation

Definition
An explanation tells the reader how or why something works or happens. It can be about natural things, e.g. *why volcanoes erupt*, or about mechanical things, e.g. *how a radio works*.

Purpose
To explain.

Text plan

1 Title

> Tells the reader what the explanation is about. Often contains *how* or *why*.

2 Introduction

> Tells the reader about the subject or process of the explanation.

3 A paragraph describing the parts and/or appearance of the subject or process to be explained

4 A paragraph explaining what something does, or why or how it works, often in time order

5 Concluding paragraph

> Summarising or rounding off. This could include where the subject or process occurs, or its effects.

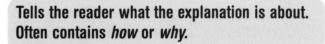

Language features
Use PRESENT TENSE verbs, e.g. *Ships carry goods.* Use PAST TENSE verbs for historical topics, e.g. *Pirate ships were common.*

Use TIME-BASED CONNECTIVES to show the order in which things happen, e.g. *first, next, finally.*

Use CAUSE AND EFFECT CONNECTIVES to show how one thing makes something else happen, e.g. *as, so that, in order to, because, this results in.*

Use TECHNICAL VOCABULARY (specific language for the subject), e.g. *When the wind blows, the angle of the sails make the ship tack.*

EXPLAIN technical terms if need be. You can define terms in the text, or write a glossary, e.g. *tack: sail into the wind using a zig-zag pattern.*

Typical style
The PASSIVE VOICE, e.g. *Sometimes travellers were captured by pirates*, can make the explanation more formal. Remember to use a variety of sentence types.

Tip	★ Explanations can be in the form of letters, diagrams, information leaflets, encyclopaedia entries and posters.

Text example

How pirates attack! (from *How to be a successful pirate!*)

Pirate ships attack any merchant vessel they think might contain valuable goods or money. If the pirate ship is a well-armed large vessel this does not present a problem, but in reality, pirate ships are not big or well armed.

So how can a small pirate ship overcome a larger vessel that has superior fire-power and a crew that outnumbers them? The main tactics used by pirates should be speed and surprise.

When a ship is seen in the distance, the pirate captain studies it through his telescope and makes an assessment of how far away it is and what booty it contains. He then orders the crew to set the sails to make maximum speed towards the vessel. When the pirates are closer to the target, they slow down and attempt to fool the larger vessel into thinking their ship is harmless. Often they raise the same flag so they appear to come from the same country. Sometimes they even send a distress message using the ship's flags. When the pirates are so close that the other ship cannot escape, they throw off their disguise and raise the Jolly Roger.

Even then, you might think, a ship with a much larger crew and armed with many more cannons would easily be able to resist the attack. Therefore, in order to overcome larger, better armed ships, pirates rely heavily on fear! They swarm onto the deck of the target, shouting and screaming, firing guns with clouds of smoke and creating as much noise and chaos as possible. The famous pirate 'Blackbeard' even has lighted fuses tied in his hair. He looks so fearsome that often crews surrender without putting up any fight at all. All this quick action usually means that the captured crew are defeated.

Next, the Pirate captain offers a deal to the captives: they can join the pirates or be thrown overboard! It is not surprising that many captured seamen become pirates themselves.

Practice questions

1 You have invented a system to stop pirates from being able to board ships. Shipping companies that have lost their cargo to pirates want to know all about it. Write an article for *Shipping Magazine* explaining how it works.

This is a **long** writing task, so you have 45 minutes to plan, write and check your writing.

2 Your class has invented a new type of lunch box! Write a letter from your teacher to the parents of your class, explaining how this works.

This is a **short** writing task, so you have 20 minutes to plan, write and check your writing.

HOW DID YOU DO?

Now go back and check your work!

1. This task was to write an explanation in the form of a magazine article. The audience would be the owners of shipping companies, so the article would be formal in style. Did you use paragraphs? Did you use cause and effect language? If you have used past tense verbs, then it has turned into a recount! If you wrote telling the shipping companies how to work the system themselves, then it has turned into instructions!

2. This task was to write an explanation in the form of a letter from your teacher to the parents. (See page 62 for an example answer.)

Discussion

Achieved?
:) :| :(

Definition

A discussion text or *balanced argument* gives the reader information about an issue from different points of view. Readers are left to make up their own minds about how they feel about the issue.

Purpose

To present opposing points of view about an issue.

Text plan

1 Title — Often in the form of a question.

2 Identifying the issue — Opening paragraph states and explains what the issue is and briefly introduces the main arguments.

3 Points in support of the issue — Arguments for, with supporting evidence.

4 Points opposing the issue — Arguments against, with supporting evidence. You can also use argument/counter-argument, one point at a time.

5 Concluding paragraph — Summarising or rounding off. This sometimes recommends one point of view.

Language features

You can use PRESENT TENSE verbs or the PAST TENSE depending on the issue.

Use LOGICAL CONNECTIVES to organise your argument, e.g. *therefore, consequently, so.*

Use connectives that show the OPPOSITE view, e.g. *on the one hand, on the other hand, but, however, nevertheless.*

Use a CONNECTIVE in the final paragraph to signal that you are SUMMING UP, e.g. *in conclusion, to summarise, finally.*

Use EVIDENCE and EXAMPLES to support the points made. These could be numbers and statistics, facts or quotes.

Typical style

Use an IMPERSONAL STYLE. Say what <u>people</u> think, not what <u>you</u> think. Use the PASSIVE VOICE, e.g. *It is thought that, it is believed.*

Challenge

Find and list the passive verb phrases in the discussion on page 19.

Tip ★ Remember to keep your argument balanced. Write four or five points for, and four or five points against.

Text example

How should pirates be punished?

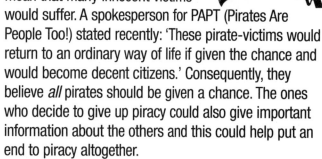

Everyone agrees that piracy is the greatest problem to our merchant ships this century. Pirates plunder our ships, steal their cargoes, capture our sailors and frequently kill them. Everybody involved in sea-travel seems to have a horror story about pirates.

Recently, there has been a great deal of publicity about what to do to about it. It seems most people think any pirates that are caught should immediately be hanged. People argue that this would act as a warning to others. It would show the young, the poor, beggars and thieves that piracy only leads to one outcome – death. They also argue that pirates don't deserve anything else.

However, there are others who believe that *everyone* has the right to a trial. It is a well-known fact that many seamen have been forced to become pirates when they were themselves captured. The number of unwilling pirates is believed to be as high as 45%. Therefore, hanging pirates without a trial could mean that many innocent victims would suffer. A spokesperson for PAPT (Pirates Are People Too!) stated recently: 'These pirate-victims would return to an ordinary way of life if given the chance and would become decent citizens.' Consequently, they believe *all* pirates should be given a chance. The ones who decide to give up piracy could also give important information about the others and this could help put an end to piracy altogether.

On the other hand, most people believe such a soft approach would result in more pirates, not fewer.

It has been shown that swift and strong punishment has led to a reduction in petty theft by pick-pockets and others. This may also prove to be the case with piracy.

Whatever the final conclusion, it is clear that this issue is complex and needs detailed discussion by Parliament before a solution can be found.

Practice questions

There has been a huge increase in the amount of graffiti on the streets of your town. Some examples of the graffiti are beautifully drawn and coloured, others are just scribble. Your task is to write a TV news report to prompt discussion about what should be done, both to the graffiti artists and to the graffiti itself.

This is a **long** writing task, so you have 45 minutes to plan, write and check your writing.

Write a summary using bullet points to help a speaker set the scene for a discussion on 'Should mobile phones be allowed in school?'

This is a **short** writing task, so you have 20 minutes to plan, write and check your writing.

HOW DID YOU DO?

Now go back and check your work!

1. This task was to write a discussion in the form of a TV news report. The audience is the general public, so your writing should be fairly formal. Even though it would be a spoken news report, the issue is important to the audience, so did you organise your points clearly in paragraphs? Did you

2. This task was to write a discussion in bullet point form to summarise the issue and provide someone with notes about it. Did you identify the issue? Did you write your points briefly, but remember to give some supporting evidence? (See page 62 for an example answer.)

balance points for and against the issue?

Persuasion

Definition
A persuasive text tries to make the reader think, do or buy something.

Purpose
To persuade.

Text plan

1 Identify the main point of the text

Could be a statement or question to grab the reader's attention.

2 Supporting points

Organise the reasons into a paragraph for each point with supporting evidence. Explain how people are being affected by the situation.

3 Summary of key points

Repeat the key points to reinforce them.

4 Call to action

Ask the reader to take some action, e.g. to do something, to buy something, to think something, to go somewhere.

Language features
Normally the PRESENT TENSE is used, but you could move into the past or future depending on the point being made.

Support the reasons with EVIDENCE. This could be numbers and statistics, facts or quotes.

Appeal to your readers' emotions by using EMOTIVE LANGUAGE. Make them think about how what you are saying affects them. Try to make them feel something with words, e.g. *It all costs money and who pays for it? You do!*

Include lots of detail in order to explain your ideas clearly and you will be more persuasive.

Typical style
Use the PASSIVE VOICE if you don't want to say where you are getting your evidence from, e.g. *It is thought ... It is believed ... Studies have shown ...*

Challenge
How many passive verb phrases can you find in the text on page 21? If you can use one or two passive verbs, you will get better marks, but don't overdo it!

Tip
★ Persuasive texts can be in virtually any form. They can be letters, posters, leaflets, newspaper and magazine articles or adverts. Remember to think about the *purpose* of the text. Remember to think about who the *audience* is and which words you choose.

Text example

Dear Mr Jones,

I am writing to complain about the quality of the school dinners on offer recently at St Starvin's Primary School.

There have been no fresh fruit or vegetables offered for the last two weeks. Also the chips and nuggets are always very greasy and unappetising. The standard of desserts is also poor – we have had prunes and semolina every day for a month.

As a result of this a number of Year 6 pupils have refused to eat their lunch and have been tired and unable to concentrate in the afternoons.

It has been proven that five portions of fresh fruit and vegetables should be eaten every day to keep people healthy, particularly children. Studies have also shown that protein eaten at lunch time has the effect of boosting brain-power for the rest of the day. Our National Tests begin in May and many of us are very concerned that our results will suffer as a result of this poor diet! This, of course, would have a very bad effect on the reputation of the school.

Although a small number of pupils enjoy your fried food, the majority of us are keen to maintain a balanced diet and lead a healthy lifestyle.

Could you please provide us with suggestions for alternative menus? A group of us would be happy to help with this as we have many ideas ourselves.

I look forward to hearing from you soon.

Yours sincerely,

Em T. Tum, Class 6D

Practice questions

(1) Your class has been told that there won't be any school trips for them this year, due to lack of funds. Write a letter to the school governors to persuade them to hold more fundraising events.

This is a **long** writing task, so you have 45 minutes to plan, write and check your writing.

(2) Your school football team is short of players. Write a poster to advertise a try-out session after school.

This is a **short** writing task, so you have 20 minutes to plan, write and check your writing.

HOW DID YOU DO?

Now go back and check your work!

1. This task was to write a persuasive text in the form of a letter. The audience was the school governors. This means that the tone of the letter should be formal. You need to have thought carefully about your point of view and how to appeal to the governors, and supported your point of view with reasons and evidence. Did you organise your letter into paragraphs? Did you reinforce your main point by repetition? Did you ask the governors to take action?

2. This task was to write a persuasive text in the form of a poster. The audience was other children in your school so the tone could be informal. Did you include key information and brief language? Did you remember to attract the readers' attention and use language that appealed to the audience?
(See page 62 for an example answer.)

Writing fiction

Fiction texts can be in the form of stories, plays or poetry. The main purpose of fiction is to entertain a reader. It can also make readers think about a theme or an issue, or teach a lesson or moral.

In this section we will concentrate on writing stories.

There are three things that all stories have in common:

Setting   Characters   Theme

Page 23 of this book looks at the way stories are structured.

Page 24 looks at these story 'ingredients'. You need to put all three into the mixture to make a story.

There is a section on each of the ingredients on pages 25–28. Each section provides you with tips, ideas and examples. There are also some practice questions. These are short writing tasks.

Stories need planning! On pages 30 and 31 you will find ideas to help you plan. Planning is important, so don't skip this bit!

Over to you!
- Work through each section carefully.
- Make sure you understand what you want your reader to think or feel.
- Have a go at the practice questions.
- Look back at the section. Have you included the right sort of detail in the right sort of way?

Achieve Level 4 Writing
At Level 4 your writing is lively and thoughtful. You can develop your ideas and organise them according to the purpose of your writing. You can make adventurous choices of vocabulary and use words for effect. You can use a variety of sentence types including complex sentences, and your spelling and punctuation is usually accurate. Your handwriting is fluent, joined and legible.

Tips	★ All writers 'borrow' ideas from other writers, so read as much as you can! Note down ideas, sentences, phrases and words that you like. Use them in your own writing.
	★ Keep a 'writing ideas' book.
	★ Your reader doesn't know what is happening inside your head while you write, so make sure you tell or show them.
	★ When your characters are talking, tell the reader who is speaking.
	★ Use paragraphs. Think *Person, Time, Place* (PTP). When the person, time or place changes in your story, start a new paragraph.

Story structure

All stories are organised in the same basic way.

When you plan your story, think in five sections:

1 Beginning — **Introduce the setting and the main characters.**

2 Build-up — **The story gets going. The characters start to do something.**

3 Problem — **Something goes wrong! This is the most exciting part of the story.**

4 Resolution — **The problem gets sorted out.**

5 Ending — **All the loose ends are tied up. The characters think or reflect on what has happened.**

Setting, characters and theme

Before you plan your story, you need to decide on the three main ingredients: setting, characters and theme.

Setting

This is WHEN and WHERE your story takes place. You need to help your readers make a picture in their minds. The setting can also be used to create an atmosphere and affect how the reader feels.

Think about some of the stories you have read. When and where were they set? How do you know? Look at some short stories to see how the authors have told the reader about the setting. Have a go at drawing the setting that you read about.

There is more about story settings on page 25.

Characters

This is WHO is in the story. You need to help the readers build up a picture of the characters – not just APPEARANCE but also PERSONALITY. Your readers need to have an idea of what the characters are like.

Think about the stories you have read. Who were the characters? What were they like? How do you know? What were they called? How did they speak? Look at some short stories to see how authors have told the reader about the characters. Try drawing a character as you see them in your mind's eye.

There is more about character on page 26 and more about dialogue (how characters speak) on page 29.

Theme

This is WHAT happens in the story. Some people say that there are only a few story themes in the world. All writers borrow ideas from other stories and this is something you can do.

Think about stories you have read. What happened? Did one story remind you of any others? List some of the common themes, e.g. good overcomes evil, main character loses something.

There is more about theme on page 28.

Once you have chosen your ingredients, mix them together and make a story!

Setting

Introduce the setting in the beginning section of the story. Remember, the two things you need to tell your readers are *when* and *where* the story is set.

When and where?

The big picture
Is your story set in the past, now or in the future? Look at these three examples. How has the writer told the reader about the big picture?

The spaceship hovered near the planet, waiting for cargo-ships to leave the surface.

Black Jake stuffed his cutlass through his belt, straightened his tricorn hat and began to stride across the quarter deck.

Jon eagerly put his new Harry Potter DVD into the player and pressed Play.

Above, this writer has used objects to tell us when and where the story is set. Spaceships and planets point to the story being set in the future. A cutlass, tri-corn hat and quarter deck tell us this story is probably set in the past. The DVD shows us that the story is set in the present day.

The smaller picture
Writers tell us more about the setting by adding smaller details. Look how the writer tells us about the season when the story takes place.

Twists of dust rose in the heat of the planet's surface as it moved towards the blazing sun.

Black Jake shielded his eyes as the snowflakes grew thicker and peered into the murky distance.

Jon settled down to enjoy the next hour and ignored the rain and wind as they lashed the last of the leaves from the trees outside.

This is a more interesting way than just saying *It was very hot ...* or *It was a cold winter day ...* or *On a wet autumn afternoon ...*

Characters

Introduce your main characters at the beginning of the story. Have a picture of them in your mind. Three things that will make your characters 'real' are:

• what they look like
• what they say and how they say it
• how they move.

What they look like

You can describe the characters' face, hair and clothes.

What do you think the two characters below are like? How has the writer made you feel that way?

> Jack strode to the window, his long black coat flapping around his strong legs. A deep frown creased his forehead and his eyes narrowed dangerously beneath the brim of his hat.

> Her wild tangled hair was only half-tamed by the bits of twine tied into it. Her clothes had seen better days; torn striped breeches and an old lace shirt; but she stood straight and tall as any great lady of society.

Challenge 1

The descriptions above tell us something about the characters' appearance. What else has the writer told us about these characters?

Tip	★ Make sure your descriptions are *important* to your character. Don't waste words when they are not needed in the story!

What they say and how they say it

Dialogue adds interest and variety to your writing. But dialogue needs to move the story along. What has the writer done in these two extracts?

> Jack strode to the window, his long black coat flapping around his strong legs. A deep frown creased his forehead and his eyes narrowed dangerously beneath the brim of his hat. 'Who laughed?' he growled angrily.

> Her wild tangled hair was only half-tamed by the bits of twine tied into it. Her clothes had seen better days; torn striped breeches and an old lace shirt; but she stood straight and tall as any great lady of society. 'Stay where you are!' she cried, her voice trembling.

The writer has added dialogue that tells us what the characters said, but also how they said it by using powerful speech verbs and adverbs.

How they move

Describing how the characters move helps to bring your writing to life. What words has the author used in the extracts above to describe the movement of the

characters?

Challenge 2

Write a paragraph describing in your own words how you feel about each of these two characters. Look for *clues* in the descriptions. Think about:
- Appearance – why do they look the way they do?
- Dialogue – what does the dialogue tell you about each character's feelings and personality?
- Movement – what does the way they move tell you about the characters?

Tips	★ Keep to two or three characters only. If you have two characters, make one male and one female, then there is no confusion about pronouns (*he/she*). ★ Only use dialogue when it tells the reader more about the character or the plot. Don't waste words on idle chat. ★ Don't tell your reader everything. Give clues!

Practice questions

1 Old Ben is a very old sailor who is grumpy. His age and experience make him short-tempered with younger sailors. Write a description of how he eats his breakfast on the deck of a busy ship. Remember to give readers clues through action, appearance and dialogue. Give clues – don't tell. Include details about what else is happening around him as he eats, and how he shows his grumpiness and short temper with the younger sailors.

This is a **long** writing task, so you have 45 minutes to plan, write and check your writing.

2 Your best friend is an astronaut. Write a description of her when you meet her as she lands from her latest space mission.

This is a **short** writing task, so you have 20 minutes to plan, write and check your writing. Use the space below to plan your answers.

27

Theme

Most stories have simple themes:
- Good beats bad
- Lost and found
- Wishing or wanting.

Challenge 1

Which theme do you think belongs to these well-known stories? Discuss your answers with friends or your teacher.

- *The Lord of the Rings*

- *Harry Potter*

- *Cinderella*

Basic structure
Good overcomes evil.

 **1** Beginning — Two characters – one good, one evil. Setting.

2 Build-up — Evil character plots against good character. Good character is innocently unaware.

3 Problem — Evil character tricks or threatens to harm good character.

4 Resolution — Good character outwits evil character.

5 Ending — Everything is OK. Characters reflect or think about what has happened.

Once you've got the hang of the structure you can start to experiment. You might write a story about a person overcoming a fear or a bully. It's still a similar structure.

Challenge 2

Can you use a grid like this to work out how the themes of **lost and found** and **wishing or wanting** follow the plan?

Now try it with other stories you know.

Dialogue

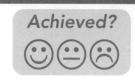

A story without any dialogue could be very dull. *What* characters say and *how* they say it can tell readers a lot about the characters in a story *and* move the plot along.

Use powerful speech verbs to tell your readers about the character who is speaking.

Consider these examples:
1. *The stranger stood in front of me. 'Move,' he muttered.*
2. *The stranger stood in front of me. 'Move!' he shouted.*
3. *The stranger stood in front of me. 'Move,' he pleaded.*
4. *The stranger stood in front of me. 'Move!' he screamed.*

How do the different speech verbs affect your thoughts:
a) about the character of the stranger?
b) about the plot?

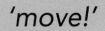

'move...'

'Move!'

'move!'

Challenge

Write a sentence to suggest why 'the stranger' said '*Move*' in each of the four different ways.

'Said' is the speech verb that is used the most but it doesn't tell readers anything about character or plot. Use it when you do not need to add extra detail.

Try to use a variety of powerful and common speech verbs. Don't overuse powerful verbs.

Tips	★ Dialogue needs to move the story along. Only use it when you want to tell the reader something important about the setting, characters or plot.
	★ Try to use a variety of verbs *and* adverbs to show how characters are speaking.

Grammar and punctuation in dialogue

Make it very clear who is speaking. When a new person joins the dialogue, always start their spoken words on a new line.

Use pronouns (*he/she/they*) and the characters' names. See pages 39–40 for further information about punctuation and punctuating dialogue.

Planning

Planning is a very useful way of thinking about story ingredients and organising your ideas. In the KS2 long writing task, you only have about 10 minutes' planning time ... not very long at all! So you need to develop a way of planning that is fast and that works for you.

Try using the five-box plan below. Make sure you know the heading for each box and the main things that need to be in that section of the story.

Heading	Main things to include	Example
Beginning	Introduce main character	Joe, boy about 11, into skateboarding.
	Setting	Old empty house, bit spooky.
Build-up	Story gets going	Joe goes into house. Looking for something. Sees paw prints.
Problem	Something goes wrong	Can hear cat but can't get to it. Cat stuck behind wall.
Resolution	Problems sorted out	Joe finds secret button to open wall. Rescues cat.
Ending	Loose ends tied up Characters reflect or think	Everything OK. Joe and cat go off on skateboard.

Now it's just a case of turning your plan into a story. But please remember to refer to your plan while you are writing – don't write something completely different!

1. Practise quickly drawing out the five-box plan and adding the headings. This should take no more than 30 seconds!
2. Now look back at the main things to include. Practise adding the main things to your five boxes. This should take another 30 seconds.
3. Next, practise planning actual stories (you don't need to write them at this stage). Look at some of the long tasks on page 31. Read the task carefully, then reread it. Got an idea? Go!
4. Think about the story ingredients you could include. Remember – **setting, characters, theme**. Spend no more than 4 minutes on this. You've now used up 5 minutes of your planning time.
5. Make notes about the ingredients in the boxes. Remember, these are notes, not sentences! You are not writing the story here – you are planning it. Five minutes later – time's up!

Tips	★ Read the task carefully first. Then make notes. Think *setting, characters, theme*. Don't write sentences – you are not writing the story yet, just making a plan. Your plan will not be marked. Then stick to your plan. ★ A well-planned story will get much better marks than one that rambles and ends abruptly.

Putting it all together

So, you know the three story ingredients (setting, characters, theme), you know the structure and you know how to plan (five-box plan). It's just a case of putting it all together in a short story.

Remember, in the long writing task you have 10 minutes of planning time and 35 minutes of writing time. This is not very long. You can't afford to have too much detail or make the characters have great adventures. Keep it simple!

Look at the example below. It's about the right length and includes all the story ingredients that you have been reading about.

Tip	★ Make sure you plan the ending for your writing! You will lose marks if you run out of time before showing you can plan the WHOLE story.

The empty house

Joe pushed open the huge wooden door into a large stone-floored hallway. He slipped through the doorway, cobwebs brushing his face. Once inside he breathed in the musty, damp smell of the old empty house.

'Hello!' he called. 'Is anyone there?' All he heard was his own voice echoing around the hall. Looking at the floor he could see paw prints in the dust. He moved forward, tracking them like a hunter in the desert. Then, suddenly, they stopped. Joe found himself staring at a blank wall. There were no more paw prints to be seen.

'Cinders can't have disappeared into thin air,' he muttered. 'Cats don't do that.'

He paused and held his breath. He thought he could hear a faint meowing. He listened hard. His black eyes stood out in his pale face as he knelt down on the floor and put his ear to the wall. Finally his face brightened as he started tapping at the wall.

With a creak, a panel in the wall started to move. The meowing grew louder and Joe's smile grew wider. Eventually the gap in the wall was big enough to reveal … Cinders, Joe's little black cat.

'Oh Cinders, how did you get in there?' asked Joe. Cinders arched her back and purred.

'Come on, let's go,' Joe said. He picked up his skateboard as the pair left the empty house. Placing it on the ground, he patted the front. Cinders jumped on and sat up straight, looking like the proudest cat in town. Joe hopped on behind her and they sped off down the street.

'That's the last time I let you go mouse hunting in there!' Joe told his cat. Cinders blinked and didn't make a sound.

Practice questions

These are **long** writing tasks, so you have 10 minutes to think and plan and 35 minutes to write and check your writing.

1. You are in a big shopping centre with your dad and little sister. Continue the story after this opening sentence, *'Where's little Mari?' asked Dad …*

2. Write a story with this title: 'The mystery of the missing garden gnome'.

3. Write a story that could end with this sentence: *'Jamal knew that Butch Brown would never scare him again.'*

4. Write a story with these ingredients: a black cat, an old woman, a scary wood, good overcomes evil.

5. Write a story about a girl who wants to star in the school play.

Sentences

Now you know how to organise your writing for non-fiction and for stories, you know what to include and what to leave out.

> Polishing up your grammar could make the final difference to your writing.

In a Level 4 piece of writing, the writer needs to:
- use different types of SENTENCE and PUNCTUATE them correctly
- organise writing into PARAGRAPHS
- use a variety of suitable CONNECTIVES
- choose VOCABULARY carefully.

Tip	★ When you are reading, look carefully at how writers use grammar. Remember, you can 'borrow' their ideas and use them in your own writing.

Remember, to achieve Level 4 you need to use different types of sentence and punctuate them correctly.

- Sentences start with a capital letter and end with a full stop (.), question mark (?) or exclamation mark (!).

- A sentence is made up of one or more clauses.

- There are three main types of sentence – simple, compound and complex. You can use them in different ways to have an effect on your reader.

Three types of sentence

Simple sentences
As the name suggests, simple sentences are easy to write and read. They have one clause: *It was raining.*

Using lots of simple sentences can be very boring for a reader.

I went out. It was raining hard. I put up my brolly. I saw my friend Daisy. I called loudly to her. She came over.

These sentences aren't very interesting for a reader because they are all the same length.

Challenge 1
Can you write your own simple sentence?

I will go to the shop.

Compound sentences
Compound sentences have two or more clauses that are as important as each other. They can be joined by these connectives:

and   but   so

It was raining hard <u>so</u> I put up my brolly.

Tips	★ Be careful that you don't always use *and* to join two clauses. ★ Learn the connectives in the list so that you can use all of them.

Challenge 2
Can you make your simple sentence into a compound sentence?

I will go to the shop and bye a bag of chips

Complex sentences
Complex sentences have two or more clauses, but one clause is more important than the others. This is called the *main clause*. A less important clause is called a *subordinate clause*. A subordinate clause is linked to the main clause by a connective:

E.g.   *after   although   as   because   before   if   in case*
       once   since   though   unless   until   when   while

When I left the house, I found it was raining hard so I put up my brolly.

Challenge 3
Try making your compound sentence into a complex sentence.

I will go to the shop and bye a bag of chips although it was £4.00

Mixing sentences

If you always use the same type of sentence, your writing will become boring. You need to use a mix.

Look again at these simple sentences.

I went out. It was raining hard. I put up my brolly. I saw my friend Daisy. I called loudly to her. She came over.

How can they be improved?

I went out. It was raining hard so I put up my brolly. As I was struggling with the catch, I saw my friend Daisy. I called loudly to her. She came over, splashing through the puddles on her way.

Well, that sounds better, doesn't it? Can you spot what's changed? Changing the sentence type means that the reader is given more detail, too.

Using questions
You can have your characters asking questions when they are speaking, but try asking questions in other parts of the story as well.

- *Hanif could just see something through the mist, but what was it?*
- *Why was the table shaking?*
- *How would Jake get out of this fix?*
- *Where were they to go now?*

Asking questions means that the reader asks them too and becomes more interested in the story.

Using exclamations
You can have your characters exclaiming when they speak. You can also use exclamations to make part of a story more interesting.

- *It spoke!*
- *She was stuck!*
- *He jumped!*
- *I was dumbstruck!*

How do they do it?

Let's look at how two children's authors use different sentence types.

The locket

He didn't look back. He set sail into the night, delighted with his daring exploits and laughing with excitement at the thought of the riches he knew would be his. Halfway into his voyage home, he could contain himself no longer and he opened the locket.

The author has used all three sentence types in this extract.

Secrets and eyes

My thirst satisfied, I looked down at the boy in faded Bermuda shorts who had taken my money. He looked at me cautiously with eyes that held the secrets of someone twice his age.

In this extract the author starts a sentence with a subordinate clause.

Challenge 4

Identify a simple sentence, a compound sentence and a complex sentence in the extract 'The locket'.

Practice questions

1. Using *The locket* extract, write a paragraph about the character. Write about where the character had been and what he had done.

2. Describe the contents of the locket and the character's reaction to it using a compound sentence. Use a simple sentence to keep the reader in suspense.

Challenge 5

Continue the story *Secrets and eyes* using a variety of types and lengths of sentence.

Tips	★ Look at books in your classroom and find examples of how authors use different sentence types in their writing. ★ Try using some of their sentences as models for your own writing.

35

Paragraphs

Remember, you need to organise your writing into paragraphs.

Paragraphs help writers organise their ideas and help readers to follow the story-line, argument or dialogue.

In **non-fiction**, starting a new paragraph shows the reader that the *PERSON, PLACE, TIME or TOPIC* has changed.

This means that:
- when a new subject (*PERSON, PLACE* or *TOPIC*) is introduced, you begin a new paragraph
- when *TIME* moves backward or forward, you begin a new paragraph.

In **fiction** you start a new paragraph when *PERSON, PLACE, TIME* or *TOPIC* has changed.

This means that:
- when you change the setting (*PLACE*), you begin a new paragraph
- when a new character (*PERSON*) is introduced, you begin a new paragraph
- when there is a change of speaker (*PERSON*), you begin a new paragraph
- when *TIME* moves backwards or forwards, you begin a new paragraph
- when a new event (*TOPIC*) happens, you begin a new paragraph.

Tip	★ **Think PPTT (PERSON, PLACE, TIME, TOPIC) for starting a new paragraph.**

Challenge

Look back at one or two of your favourite long writing tasks. Read them through and check that you remembered to begin a new paragraph each time there is a change in PPTT. Write a 'P' in the margin each time you *should* have started a new paragraph.

Look back at the writing you did for the practice questions. Do your paragraphs work?

Tip	★ **Read two pages of your reading book. At the end of each paragraph, make a note of the main focus. How is the writer moving the narrative on?**

Connectives

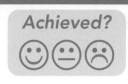
Remember, when you write you should use a variety of suitable connectives.

Connectives are words and phrases that link clauses and sentences or introduce new paragraphs.

If you look back at the non-fiction section on pages 8–19, the types of connective that you can use for different text types are listed.

> There are different connectives for different purposes.

Fiction

When you are writing stories, you usually use time-based connectives. Using *AND THEN* time after time is very boring for a reader.

Look at these suggestions for different types of time connective you could use in story writing.

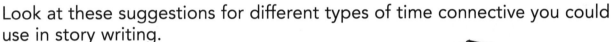

Time
We often write *THEN* or *AND THEN* or AND.

Try these instead:

Next	*When*	*Later*
Just then	*Once*	*Afterwards*
Meanwhile	*Suddenly*	*Finally*

Tip	★ When you are reading, make a note of the connectives the author has used. Think about how they have moved the story along.

Non-fiction

Addition
We often write *AND* or *AND THEN* or *THEN*.

Try these instead:

Also	*Furthermore*	*Moreover*

Against
We often write *BUT*.

Try these instead:

However	*On the other hand*	*Nevertheless*

Cause and effect
We often write *BECAUSE*.

Try these instead:

As	*In order to*	*As a result*
So	*This means that*	*This results in*
So that	*Consequently*	*This leads to*

Logical
We often write *BECAUSE* or *SO*.

Try these instead:

Therefore	*Consequently*
Furthermore	*Thus*

Summing up
We often write *FINALLY*.

Try these instead:

In conclusion	*To summarise*	*As a result*

Tips	★ Don't use the same connective over and over again in one piece of writing.
	★ Make a list of connectives and learn them.
	★ Collect new connectives from your reading.

Challenge

Use these three connectives to make compound sentences from the following simple sentences: a) *because*   b) *although*   c) *until*

1. *The attack began well. They had been warned of our approach.*
2. *The waves continued crashing on the decks. Everything below was soaked through.*
3. *He stopped running. His heart wasn't in it any more.*

Punctuation

Punctuation tells your reader *how* to read your writing.

Correct punctuation makes sense of your writing and stops your reader getting confused.

This means using FULL STOPS, QUESTION MARKS, EXCLAMATION MARKS, COMMAS, APOSTROPHES and SPEECH PUNCTUATION in the right places.

> Read these words out loud. How does the punctuation change the meaning?
>
> *Now.   Now!   Now?   Now …*

TRICKY PUNCTUATION

Commas

A comma is a punctuation mark that separates part of a sentence.
Use commas to:

1. separate names, adjectives or items in a list, e.g.
   They helped themselves to tea, coffee, milk and sugar.
   Blackbeard, Captain Kidd, Black Bess and Captain Jake are all wanted for piracy on the High Seas.
2. give extra information without affecting the sense of the sentence, e.g.
   No dogs, except guide dogs, are allowed in the Botanical Gardens.
3. separate subordinate clauses, e.g.
   In spite of the rough seas, they made a speedy crossing over the Channel.

Tips	★ You don't need to use a comma before *and*.
	★ Read your sentence aloud. It will help you to hear where the commas should go.

SPEECH PUNCTUATION

There are two ways of telling a reader what a character says: indirect speech and direct speech.

Indirect speech

This is also known as 'reported' speech, when you don't use the speakers' exact words but report what they said, e.g.

* *The Captain said that there would be extra rations for the men.*
* *The teacher threatened to give extra homework if their work did not improve.*
* *The doctor told me how she had saved his life.*

Direct speech

You can use the speaker's actual words inside speech marks (' ', or sometimes " ") but there is a bit more punctuation needed!

- The most common punctuation is a comma.
  E.g. *'We are going to have a wonderful time,' he announced.*
  Here the comma is used at the end of the spoken words INSIDE the speech marks.

- If the speaker continues speaking, you need another comma before the next spoken words.
  E.g. *'We are going to have a wonderful time,' he announced, 'and everyone will take part!'*

- If you start the sentence with the speaker and speech verb, the comma comes before the speech mark and the speech begins with a capital letter.
  E.g. *Flora said, 'You don't have to go.'*

- Full stops, exclamation marks and question marks must be placed inside the speech marks.
  E.g. *'I'm not going!' she yelled.*

- And finally – new speaker = new line.
  E.g. *'I'm not going!' she yelled.*
  'Why not?' asked Mr Parker.

Tips	★ Notice that when the speech verb comes in the middle of one continuous sentence, the second group of words inside speech marks do *not* need a capital letter to begin them.
	★ The speech verb or pronoun after the spoken word always begins with a lowercase letter, while a PROPER NOUN begins with a capital, e.g.
	• *'Rubbish,' she said.*
	• *'Rubbish!' answered Mary.*
	• *'Rubbish,' Mary cried.*
	★ If the spoken words end with an exclamation mark or with a question mark, you still use a lowercase letter after the speech mark.

Apostrophes

Take special care with apostrophes! They can change the meaning of a sentence when used badly.

There are only two reasons why you need an apostrophe:
* to show that something belongs to somebody (possession)
* to show that a letter or letters have been missed out (omission).

Possession

The boy's homework shows that the homework belongs to the boy.

Be careful with plural nouns (more than one).
The boy's boots means the boots belonging to one boy.
The boys' boots means the boots belonging to two or more boys.

Omission

Sometimes a letter (or part of a word) is missed out to make a shortened form.

This often occurs in direct speech so that it sounds natural.
Could not becomes *Couldn't*   *Was not* becomes *Wasn't*
Captain can become *Cap'n*

Tips	★ **It** – this is the really tricky one. Learn the rule and you won't make mistakes! ★ **The apostrophe is ONLY EVER used when a letter is missed out (the shortened form).** E.g. *It is a great adventure* becomes *It's a great adventure.* ★ **The apostrophe is NEVER EVER used to show possession with** it. ★ **NEVER EVER use an apostrophe with plural nouns UNLESS it shows possession.**

Practice question

Read the passage below. All the punctuation has been stolen, even all the capital letters and full stops! Your challenge is to put it back in. Read the passage carefully and out loud before you start and you will see how important punctuation is to readers.

The ship had been becalmed before but never for so long some of the men lay about the decks that baked in the heat others stayed below hoping for cooler air but the smell of so many men in a small space soon sent them on deck again was that a breath of wind asked the first mate hopefully perhaps it was said capn jake i think youre right all hand to the sails he cried his voice reaching all through the tiny ship men women and children went scurrying aloft

Tip
There are:

9 capital letters	7 full stops	5 commas
2 apostrophes	3 sets of speech marks	1 question mark
1 exclamation mark		

Check your answer against the punctuated passage on page 63.

Vocabulary

Think about the words you are going to use in your writing. If you choose them well they can improve the standard of your writing. They can give your reader a clear picture of what you mean and you will get your message across.

Remember, try to avoid repeating favourite words in a single piece of writing.

ADJECTIVES

Adjectives are used to describe a noun. They describe something or someone, e.g.
A red door.
A crying child.

Tips	★ Avoid using adjectives that say the same thing, e.g. *A frozen icy lake.* Instead, use two adjectives that say something different, e.g. *A vast icy lake.* ★ Avoid using adjectives in writing that you use when chatting, e.g. *really, very, nice, OK.* *We all ate a really nice meal* is dull. *We all ate a delicious meal* is better.	★ Adjectives that have the same initial sound as the noun work well in poetry and fiction. This is called alliteration, e.g. *The magical music.* ★ Remember, only use factual adjectives in non-fiction. Use them to add information, e.g. *The white football* rather than *the gloriously gleaming white football.*

Challenge 1

Change the adjectives in upper case to give readers a better picture in their mind's eye:

Wonderful
1. This is a GOOD story.
2. The train had NICE purple doors.
3. After the race his face was VERY RED.
4. Mrs Lane is REALLY CROSS.
5. The tree had BIG flowers on its branches.

Adverbs are used to describe a verb. They describe how something is said or done.

- *He gripped tightly.*
- *'I think so,' he answered quietly.*

Adverbs often end in 'ly'.

Challenge 2

Look again at the section on characters on page 26. In the extracts, can you find any adverbs that describe how characters speak or move?

Practice questions 1

Choose an adverb to make these sentences more interesting:

1 *He banged the book onto the table.*

2 *'You look out!' he whispered.*

3 *The monkeys climbed from branch to branch.*

4 *'It wasn't me!' she said.*

VERBS

Verbs tell us what someone or something is doing. Choose your verbs well and it can improve your writing. Which sentence do you think gives a better picture of what is happening?

Sunita put the shoe back into the box.
Sunita slammed the shoe back into the box.

Martin got his hat and raced to the door.
Martin grabbed his hat and raced to the door.

| Tip | ★ Avoid using *put* or *got*. They don't tell the reader much about what is happening. |

Practice questions 2

Choose a new verb to add interest to these sentences:

1 Hordes of menacing monkeys *swung* through the high treetops.

2 The proud princess *walked* along the streets of cheering crowds.

3 She *put* the china cups carefully in the basket.

4 The thief *got* through the broken attic window.

| Tip | ★ In the National Tests you need to show that you can make good vocabulary choices. Have a go at different words. If you get the spelling wrong, you'll still get more marks for choosing good vocabulary than you lose for wrong spelling. |

Spelling

The Spelling Test lasts for 10 minutes. You will be asked to spell 20 words from a passage that your teacher reads to you.

The test will cover:
* basic spelling rules
* more difficult or unusual words that might not fit basic spelling rules.

Below is a list of the 20 most frequently misspelled words in the National Tests over the last few years. Make sure you get them right this year!

change	nastiest	technique	stripes	advertise
designed	swimming	perfectly	injured	regardless
ready	future	serious	attempts	vanishing
produce	surprise	individual	known	themselves

The spelling rules that follow will help you. Read them through and make sure you understand them. Then remember to use them when you write.

Plurals

* Most words just add *s*: *road – roads; cup – cups; book – books; cat – cats*

* Some words need *es* to be added. Say them aloud and listen to how they sound. Words that end in a hissing or buzzing sound follow this rule. Words that end in *x, z, ch, sh* and *s* also follow this pattern:
box – boxes; bus – buses; watch – watches

* Words that end in *f* have a different pattern. You usually need to drop the *f* and add *ves*: *hoof – hooves; wolf – wolves*
But beware! There are exceptions. Try to learn these words:
gulf – gulfs; roof – roofs; dwarf – dwarfs/dwarves

* Words that end in *y* have a simple rule. If the letter before *y* is a vowel (*a e i o u*), just add *s*: *way – ways; toy – toys; monkey – monkeys*
If any other letter (a consonant) comes before the *y*, drop the *y* and add *ies*:
lady – ladies; spy – spies; story – stories

* Learn the irregular words: *mouse – mice; man – men; child – children.*
When you are reading, make a note of any irregular plurals you find and learn them.

Challenge

Look through books or dictionaries and find words ending in *y, x, z* and *s*. Change them into plurals.

Practice question

Change these words into plurals:

fox, road, bunch, wish, sound, life, tax, tree, drink, pirate, house, donkey, fly, bus

DOUBLING THE CONSONANT

Adding suffixes -er, -ed or -ing

There is a simple way to understand how to spell words that end in a consonant when you add -er, -ed or -ing. Listen to the sound the vowel makes.

Vowels can make short sounds or long sounds.
Stop has a short 'o' sound.   *Boat* has a long 'o' sound.

The rule is: double the consonant when the vowel is short.
Stop – stopping   *Boat – boating*

Challenge

1. Divide these words into two lists. Put all the words with short vowel sounds in one list, and all the words with the long vowel sounds in the other list.
    bin, line, paper, chat, choose, flutter, reign, wet, meet, light, float, dot

2. Look through some books and add four new words to each list.

3. Add the ending -er, -ed or -ing to the new words to make a different word.

4. Check the vowel sound to see which words need to have a double consonant.

5. Check your spelling in a dictionary.

Quick challenge

Tenses: Put these verbs into the past, present and future tenses. It is a good way to practise many of the spelling rules. If you find spelling some of them hard, look back at the spelling rules and learn them. If you still have trouble getting them right, read as much as you can and practise all you can.

Verb	Past tense	Present tense	Future tense
To fit	I fitted I have fitted I was fitting	I fit I am fitting	I will fit
To move	I have moved	I am moving	I will move
To clap	I clapped	I'm clapping	I will clap
To keep	I keep kept	I am keeping	I will keep
To swim	I swam	I'm swimming	I will swim
To fly	I flue	I am flying	I will fly
To produce			
To try			
To pursue			

Practice questions: The spelling test

After learning all the facts and spelling rules on the previous pages, have a go at these questions. If you double your final score you will have your percentage. A good estimate for Level 4 will be over 70%. Check your answers on page 64.

Section A
Spell the plural of these words:

1. crunch [ ] **2.** aunt [ ] **3.** taxi [ ]

4. hippy [ ] **5.** werewolf [ ] **6.** lunch [ ]

7. pony [ ] **8.** chair [ ] **9.** sofa [ ]

10. hippopotamus [ ]

Section B

Correctly add 'ing' to these words:

1. bat [ ]
2. bale [ ]
3. shoot [ ]
4. weep [ ]
5. slide [ ]

Correctly add 'ed' to these words:

1. snort [ ]
2. look [ ]
3. map [ ]
4. glide [ ]
5. shop [ ]

Correctly add 'er' to these words:

1. strong [ ]
2. loud [ ]
3. big [ ]
4. white [ ]
5. bright [ ]

Section C
Read the clues then correctly spell the answers:

1. The past tense of 'break'. [ ] **2.** The past tense of 'grow'. [ ]

3. The past tense of 'sharpen'. [ ] **4.** The past tense of 'skip'. [ ]

5. Zebras and tigers have them (beginning with s). [ ] **6.** Someone who acts is an [ ].

7. It is a well k[ ] fact. **8.** The slipper fitted p[ ].

9. Ali Baba and the 40 [ ]. **10.** Elizabeth I r[ ] for 45 years.

Section D
The words in italics have been spelled incorrectly. Write down the correct spelling.

Dinosaws have been *extingt* for over 60 million years. Nobody knows *egsactly* why they died out so suddenly. Some *sientists* think a *jyant* asteroid hit the Earth and filled the atmosphere with *dence* clouds of dust. These clouds blocked the sun's rays and cold-blooded *creetures* could not *addapt* to the new conditions. However, smaller animals such as *mamals* and insects were more *addaptible* and became the new rulers of the Earth. There are still many *speesheys* which have survived from the time before the mass extinction. Crocodiles and sharks are very *sucsesfull* predators and have *exisded* on Earth for over 200 million years. We are probably more of a *thret* to the *curent* species on the planet that any impact from outer space.

Reviewing your work

Rereading or reviewing your work is an important part of being a writer. No writer thinks their work is finished without rereading it and checking that it makes sense. Don't worry if you find things that need changing – there are always changes to be made. It is a good opportunity to look at ways in which your writing could be improved.

Here are some ideas to keep in mind when you are reviewing your work.

- **Make sure your reader will understand your main message.** For example, if you are writing a mystery story, will your reader want to find out what happens? Ask yourself if you have given too many clues to the ending. Is there a feeling of suspense and excitement? If you are writing an explanation, have you used connectives to help your reader follow the process that you are explaining? Would you be able to understand the explanation easily? If you are not sure, have another look at the guidelines for writing explanations.

- **Make sure you have followed the guidelines for the text type you are writing.** If you are not sure, go back and check. Keep the style constant and try not to slip from one type of writing to another. If you have started in the first person voice, have you kept to it all the way through your writing? Have you kept to the same verb tense? Don't get worried if you find mistakes – just correct them and try to remember for the future. No one gets it right all the time, but reviewing your work helps you to spot the errors that could lose you marks.

- **Check your spelling and grammar.** Look carefully as you read and, if a word doesn't look right, try it out a few times on a piece of paper. If you can, look it up in a dictionary and try to learn the correct spelling for the future. Read your sentences aloud. This will help you to hear when something doesn't sound right. When you think your grammar is not quite right, try saying the sentence in different ways and rewrite it a few times. Pick the one that you think sounds best and don't be afraid to make changes. Go back and check for any simple mistakes. Have you added all your capital letters and full stops?

Writer's tips	★ Read as often as you can. Reading helps you become familiar with good writing, helps you remember spelling patterns and helps you learn how to structure your sentences. Read as many kinds of books as you can. This will help you get ideas for your own writing.
	★ Keep a notebook and write down ideas, phrases, sentences and words that you like. If you read a phrase that might be useful, don't be afraid to make use of it. You can learn a lot from other writers' ideas. Jot them down in your writer's notebook. You never know when they might come in handy.

Reading comprehension

ABOUT THE READING TEST

The Reading Test comes in the form of two booklets – one containing the texts you will read and another with the questions and space for your answers.

You have 1 hour for the test, including 15 minutes to read the booklets and 45 minutes to answer all the questions.

Reading the texts
Read the texts in the booklet. DON'T RUSH. Try to immerse yourself in the story or information and enjoy it.

When you have finished, take a moment to reflect and think about what you have read. What was the author's purpose? Did it make sense? Was there anything you didn't understand?

DON'T RUSH!

The questions
Always read the question carefully before you begin to write. Then you will understand what you are being asked to do.

The questions are there to test that you can:
• make sense of what you are reading
• find information and ideas in the text
• work out what the author means
• understand why a text is organised in a particular way
• comment on vocabulary and style
• say how a text makes you feel
• link what you read to your own life.

Answering the questions
Read the instructions carefully before you begin, as they give you information about how to answer the questions. DON'T RUSH! Many mistakes are made by children who do not read the question properly. You will not get any marks if you write something that does not answer the question!

Remember to REFER TO THE TEXT. You do not need to answer any questions from memory.

REFER TO THE TEXT

Reading between the lines

Authors don't always tell you exactly what is happening. They often give you clues to help you work it out for yourself.

> Josh cried long and deep into his hands. The lead hung from his pocket like a wilted flower and the hewed tennis ball was still wet from its last game with Spike. Had this actually happened? The smell of burnt tyres and the angry face of the driver told him it had.

1 What was hanging from Josh's pocket?

The answer can be found in the text itself – the lead.

2 What or who is Spike?

The text doesn't actually say, but from reading the clues (lead and chewed tennis ball) it becomes clear that Spike is a dog.

3 What has just happened?

Again, the text doesn't actually say, but you can draw your own conclusion from the text. 'The smell of burnt tyres', 'the angry face of the driver' and Josh's distress all imply that Spike has been hit by a car.

Top tips	★ Check how many marks each question is worth. 　– One mark usually means the answer is in the WORDS of the text. 　– Two or three marks usually means that you are asked to work out what the author meant – to read between the lines – or to draw on your own knowledge and experience. ★ Always answer 2- or 3-mark questions with evidence or examples from the text. ★ When a question begins *Why do you think …?* or *How do you know …?* you should always BACK UP YOUR ANSWER with examples from the text.

Achieving Level 4 reading

At Level 4, you show that you can understand a range of texts and understand their ideas, themes, events and characters. You show that you are beginning to use inference and deduction to read between the lines and can bring your own experiences into your understanding. You refer to the text when explaining your views. You can find and use ideas and information from different parts of a text.

If you can do all of these, you will achieve Level 4 and even possibly Level 5!

Text 1 (Non-fiction)

'Here be dragons!'...

The Komodo dragons are alive and well in Indonesia – not the fire-breathing winged wonders from myths and legends, but their close cousins. Here is some information about them.

Facts

Kingdom	Animalia
Class	Reptilia
Genus	*Varanus*
Size	Male length: up to 3m
	Female length: less than 2m
Weight	Males: up to 135kg
	Females: less than 50kg

Description

The Komodo dragons are the largest lizards in the world and, with their ancient appearance and evocative name, they conjure up the stuff of legends. The heavy-set body is long with stocky legs and a long muscular tail; the scaly skin is greyish-brown all over. Komodo dragons, which live on the island of Flores, however, are earthen-red in colour with a yellow head. Juveniles have a more striking pattern with highly variable combinations of bands and speckling in yellow, green, grey and brown. Their long, forked yellow tongues resemble those of the mythical, fire-breathing dragons which gave them their name.

Range

Numerous on the island of Komodo in Indonesia, from which they have received their common name, these dragons are also found on the neighbouring islands of Rinca and Flores in Indonesia.

Diet

Adult Komodo dragons are generally solitary, although groups may gather around a kill. They are powerful predators and their voracious appetite has further enhanced their ferocious image. Both carrion and live prey are consumed; adults ambush deer, water buffalo and wild pigs, and carcasses can be detected from up to 10 km away. Their large powerful jaws tear at prey and large amounts can be eaten with surprising speed. Only a small percentage of the kill is discarded. Komodo dragons can eat up to 80% of their own body weight at one time. The dragon's saliva can contain up to 50 different types of bacteria, probably as a result of eating carrion. The bite is therefore highly infectious, and even if the attacked prey escapes it is likely to die of blood poisoning within the week.

Life cycle

Komodo dragons mate during the dry season, which occurs between May and August. The males compete for the attention of the females by engaging in fierce battles. They wrestle upright, using their tails for support, grabbing each other with their front limbs and attempting to throw their opponent to the ground. The loser is the first dragon to fall.

Threats

The population of Komodo dragons today is estimated to be a mere fraction of its size 50 years ago. Causes of this decline are widespread habitat loss through the region, a loss of prey species and hunting. No Komodo dragons have been seen on the island of Padar since the 1970s, the result of widespread poaching of the deer that constitute their chief prey source.

Conservation

Komodo and surrounding islands lie within the Komodo National Park. Law has protected these dragons since the 1930s, and international trade is prohibited by their listing on Appendix 1 of the Convention on International Trade in Endangered Species (CITES). An important tourist trade has developed because of these spectacular creatures, bringing over 18,000 visitors to the area each year; it is hoped that this economic incentive will help to safeguard the future of these awesome dragons.

Tips	★ Read the text all the way through, then reread it more slowly. If you do not understand any of the vocabulary, read on through the sentence or the paragraph and see if that helps you to understand the word.
	★ When you have read it twice, think about the purpose of the text. Is it to entertain you, make you think in a certain way or give you facts and information?
	★ Read all the questions before you try to answer them. Check that you understand what each question is asking you to do.

give the meanings of : ancient, variable, resea resemble, numerous, island

Practice questions

Refer to the text when answering these questions.

1. Up to what length can a male Komodo dragon grow? *(1 mark)*
2. How does the skin colour of the dragons which live on the island of Flores differ from that of the dragons which live on Komodo? *(1 mark)*
3. On which three islands do the dragons live? *(1 mark)*
4. On what do adult dragons feed? *(1 mark)*
5. Give two reasons why prey is likely to die if attacked by a Komodo dragon. *(2 marks)*
6. Why does the author use the word 'wrestle' to describe the way in which male dragons compete for the attention of females? *(2 marks)*
7. Describe the difference between 'carrion' and 'live prey'. *(3 marks)*
8. Describe three actions that you think could be taken to halt the decline in population of the Komodo dragon. *(3 marks)*
9. Why did the author use the words 'spectacular' and 'awesome' in the last paragraph? *(3 marks)*
10. Write three ways in which Komodo dragons might be similar to dragons from myth and legend. *(3 marks)*

See page 64 for the answers.

HOW DID YOU DO?

Text 2 (Fiction)

Smile

Geraldine McCaughrean

Chapter 1

Suddenly he was falling, and his life went past in small, square pictures, framed in the windows of the cockpit. There were his family; his house, his friends, his wedding, his dog. There were pictures of the Past and pictures of the Future, too – all the things he had meant to do and now never would: bridges, faces, dawns and sunsets.

There were flames, as well, but they were not imaginary. They were running their orange tongues over the glass, licking away the views, gobbling up the sky. Flash would have liked to bid someone goodbye, but he was all alone in the plane.

The next he knew the windows were full of desert; red gulches and yellow valleys and salt-white lakes. The landscapes were so beautiful and so strange that Flash wanted to capture them, trap them like rare, free-flying birds. He wanted to photograph them.

No time for a developer and fixer. No time for darkrooms and prints. His hands closed around the only camera of any use to him.

Then the plane tilted and it was too late. The scenes framed in its windows flickered by too fast to focus upon. As a cinema film rattles free of its spool, so Flash's fall rattled to an end. The crashing aeroplane landed in a sea of grey-green trees, folding its wings upwards like a butterfly. Branches broke through the floor. Leaves burst into the cockpit. The glass windows crazed like eggshell. If Flash had not been thrown out through the shattering roof, his life would have finished then and there. The End.

He fell head-over-heart into a clump of thorn bushes. Just once his eyelids blinked, like a camera shutter, and took in the sight of his aeroplane burning, raised aloft on the arms of three blazing trees. In his head, he titled the picture 'Scorching the Sky'. Then his eyes closed and he returned to a darkroom empty of pictures, or even of dreams.

Chapter 2

'Who are you?' he asked.

'That's not hard. I know that,' said the little girl. 'What I don't know is who you are.'

She was poking long, straight branches up the legs of his trousers, and Flash felt mildly annoyed to be woken only in time to be spit-roasted.

'Olu and I, we take you home,' said the little girl. She has dusky, dusty skin the colour of milky tea, and a scarlet dress. Her long, ragged hair was dusty too. It brushed Flash's face as she pushed the branches on through his shirt and out at the collar. Then she waved to the little boy to take his place by Flash's head.

When Flash realised what they were doing, he marvelled at their cleverness. Wonderful! That these primitive people should know, so young, how to transport an injured man across hostile wilderness. They balanced something on his stomach, then they both took hold of the ends of the two branches and lifted Flash clear of the ground.

All the buttons burst from his shirt and his head hit the ground with a thud. The camera on his stomach rolled down and smacked him in the face.

'I say to Olu, I say it won't work,' said the girl, sagging under the weight of his body and legs. Any moment now she would drop him.

'Perhaps I can walk,' said Flash, feeling his trousers begin to split.

And he found he could. He was dizzy and burned, and the sun was like a kettle of hot water being poured over his aching head. But if he put one foot in front of the other and counted all the flies he passed on the way, somehow he managed to walk. The hardest thing was to tell which flies he had already counted and which were new arrivals. They all wanted to fly into his mouth.

'What's in the box?' asked the girl, pointing.

'A camera,' said Flash. 'I'm a photographer. That's what I do. Photographs.'

'Ah!' said the girl. And there was something about the empty coffee swirl of her eyes that told him instantly: she had never seen either a camera or a photographer before.

Tips	★ Read the text all the way through, then reread it more slowly. If you do not understand any of the vocabulary, read on through the sentence or the paragraph and see if that helps you understand the word.
	★ When you have read it twice, think about the purpose of the text. Is it to entertain you, make you think in a certain way or give you facts and information?
	★ Read all the questions before you try to answer them. Check that you understand what each question is asking you to do.

Practice questions

Refer to the text when answering these questions.

1. Which word in the opening paragraph tells you that he was flying in an aeroplane? *(1 mark)*

2. What did Flash entitle 'Scorching the Sky'? *(1 mark)*

3. What broke Flash's fall to the ground? *(1 mark)*

4. Write three examples of how the author uses words related to photography to describe the plane crash. *(2 marks)*

5. Find two phrases the author uses to describe the girl's appearance. *(2 marks)*

6. *'Then his eyes closed and he returned to a darkroom empty of pictures, or even of dreams.'* What does this sentence suggest happened to Flash? *(3 marks)*

7. What impression of the girl does this extract give you? Use evidence from the text to support your answer. *(3 marks)*

See page 64 for the answers.

HOW DID YOU DO?

Text 3 (Non-fiction)

Our climate!

Most of us have heard about climate change and how our planet is warming up, but have you ever stopped to think about what *you* can do about it?

Our climate is getting hotter. This is caused by something called 'the greenhouse effect'.

The earth has a natural greenhouse effect to keep us warm. Natural greenhouse gases are carbon dioxide, methane and water vapour. These gases trap the warmth generated by the sun. Without it our climate would be unable to sustain life.

In the past 200 years, humans have consumed fossil fuels at an increasing rate. This generates carbon dioxide in great quantities, which acts to trap more of the earth's heat.

The effect has been to slowly heat up the earth and the seas. The result is that we experience more extreme weather such as heavy rain and winds, which cause flooding and damage. Added to this we are destroying the planet's biggest natural defence against the effects of too much carbon dioxide – rainforests – which means more carbon dioxide given off, and less forest to absorb it.

How might this affect us?
In the short term, heavier and more intense weather will certainly lead to more flooding. In the longer term, a warmer planet will cause the polar ice caps to melt, leading to higher sea levels and increasing the risk of coastal flooding and erosion.

And this is already happening!
Did you know that by the year 2050 the sea levels in Britain will have risen by up to half a metre?

Climate change is actually changing our lives right now. It is estimated that 150,000 people around the world die each year as a direct result of climate change. Both water shortages and floods are happening! People's homes and lives are at risk.

What can you do?
Too often kids feel powerless to take any action. The issue of climate change seems too big for them to have any effect on it.

The issue is too big to ignore! We can *all* do something to reduce the amount of greenhouse gases we produce in the home.

Follow the ten point plan
1. Wearing t-shirts in winter and turning the heating up is just silly – put on warmer clothes.
2. Don't leave electrical equipment like TVs and computers on standby – they can use up to 75% of the electricity they use when turned on.
3. Take your mobile phone charger out of the socket when not being used.
4. If you don't need a full kettle of water don't boil a full kettle of water!
5. Walk or cycle to school instead of going by car.

6. Recycle!
7. Remember to turn the lights off when you leave the room ... unless somebody else is in it!

Pester power! Nag your parents to:
8. switch your electricity supply to a green tariff supplier.
9. save on their heating bill by insulating your home.
10. switch to energy efficient light bulbs. They use much less electricity and last ten times as long.

Tips	★ Read the text all the way through, then reread it more slowly. If you do not understand any of the vocabulary, read on through the sentence or the paragraph and see if that helps you understand the word. ★ When you have read it twice, think about the purpose of the text. Is it to entertain you, make you think in a certain way or give you facts and information? ★ Does the text tell you *how* we are using up fossil fuels or do you have to read between and beyond the lines by using your knowledge of the world? ★ Read all the questions before you try to answer them. Check that you understand what each question is asking you to do.

Practice questions

1 What is causing our climate to get hotter? *(1 mark)*

2 What are the three natural greenhouse gases? *(1 mark)*

3 What is the earth's biggest natural defence against the effects of carbon dioxide? *(1 mark)*

4 Why do you think that coastal flooding would result from the melting of the polar ice cap? *(2 marks)*

5 Write down two examples of where the writer has used statistics that you think are unproven (opinion rather than fact). *(2 marks)*

6 Why do you think the writer changed from 'you' to 'we' just before the ten point plan? *(3 marks)*

7 Which point on the ten point plan do you think will be easiest to do and why? *(3 marks)*

8 Why do you think the author has used direct questions? *(3 marks)*

9 Why do you think most of the ten point plan focuses on saving electricity? *(3 marks)*

See page 64 for the answers.

HOW DID YOU DO?

Text 4 (Fiction)

Alone on a Wide Wide Sea

Michael Morpurgo

Kookaburras, Cockatoos and Kangaroos

Marty didn't shout back and scream. He didn't jump up and down. Marty, I discovered, had his own very individual way of dealing with authority. He spoke very quietly, perfectly politely, fixing the man with a steady stare. 'We're staying together, Mister,' he said. And we did too, which was why I found myself later that morning sitting beside Marty on a bus, heading out of Sydney and into open country. There were ten of us on that bus, all boys, and as I looked around me I was relieved to see that only one of the boys from my cabin was there. It was Wes Snarkey, the one Marty had thumped that day on deck – he's never given me any trouble since, so that didn't bother me. Lady Luck had smiled on me – that's what I thought at the time anyway.

The driver, who seemed a chatty, cheerful sort of bloke, told us he was taking us to Cooper's Station, a big farm over 300 miles away. It would take us all day to get there. Best to settle down and sleep, he said. But we didn't. None of us did. There was too much to look at, too many wonders I'd never seen before. For a start there were the wide open spaces, hardly a house in sight, hardly any people either. But that wasn't all that amazed me that first day in Australia. All the animals and birds were as different and strange to us as the country itself. The bus driver told us what they were – and it turned out their names were as odd as they were themselves – kookaburras and cockatoos and kangaroos and possums. They didn't even have the same trees we had back home in England. They had gum trees and wattle trees instead. This wasn't just a different country we were in, it was more like a different planet. And the scrubby surface of this planet seemed to go on and on, flat on every side as far as the horizon, which shimmered blue and brown and green. And the towns we drove through were like no towns I'd ever seen before. They had great wide dusty streets, and all the houses were low. If you saw another car it was a surprise.

I was hot and dusty and thirsty on that bus, and I thought the journey would never end, but I was happy. I was happy to have arrived, happy not to be sea-sick any more. Tired though we were, we were buoyed up by the excitement of it all. This was a new adventure in a new world. We were on a bus ride into wonderland and we were loving it, every single moment of it.

Evening was coming on by the time we got to Cooper's Station, but we could still see enough. We could see it was a place on its own, way out in the bush, and we could tell it was a farm. I mean you could smell it straightaway, the moment we clambered off the bus. There were huge sheds all around, and you could hear cattle moving and shifting around inside. And further away in the gloom there was the sound of a running creek, and ducks quacking raucously. A gramophone record was playing from the nearby farmhouse, which had a tin roof and a verandah all around it. I thought at first that was where we'd all be living, but we were led past it, carrying our suitcases, down a dirt track and into a compound with a fence all around. In the centre of this was a long wooden shed with steps at one end and a veranadah.

'Your new home,' the man told us, opening the door. I didn't take much notice of him, not then, I was too busy looking around me. The gramophone needle got stuck as I stood there. I can never think of Cooper's Station without that stuttering snatch of a hymn repeating itself remorselessly in my head, 'What a friend we have in Jesus, have in Jesus, have in Jesus.' I wasn't to know it then, but it was the eerie overture that heralded the darkest years of my life.

Tips	★ Read the text all the way through, then reread it more slowly. If you do not understand any of the vocabulary, read on through the sentence or the paragraph and see if that helps you understand the word.
	★ When you have read it twice, think about the purpose of the text. Is it to entertain you, make you think in a certain way or give you facts and information?
	★ Read all the questions before you try to answer them. Check that you understand what each question is asking you to do.

Practice questions

1. What is the name of the farm they were going to? *(1 mark)*

2. What sort of trees did they see? *(1 mark)*

3. How long had the boy recounting the events been in Australia? *(1 mark)*

4. Before the bus journey to Cooper's Station, the boy had taken a different journey. What sort of journey was it and how do you know? *(2 marks)*

5. Why do you think the boy felt excited? *(2 marks)*

6. Do you think the boy was happy at Cooper's Station? Give two reasons for your answer. *(3 marks)*

See page 64 for the answers.

HOW DID YOU DO?

Text 5 (Poetry)

Ten things found in a wizard's pocket

A dark night.

Some words that nobody could ever spell.

A glass of water, full to the top.

A large elephant.

A vest made from spiders' webs.

A handkerchief the size of a car park.

A bill from the wand shop.

A bucket full of stars and planets, to mix with the dark night.

A bag of magic mints you can suck for ever.

A snoring rabbit.

Ian McMillan

Tip	★ Read each poem all the way through once and think 'What was it about?', then reread it more slowly and look for clues. Was your first impression right?

Counting the stars

It's late at night
and John is counting the stars

He's walking through the woods
and counting the stars.

The night is clear
and the stars are like salt

on a black table cloth.
John counts silently,

his lips moving, his head tilted.
It's late at night

and John is counting the stars
until he walks into a tree

that he never saw
because he was counting the stars.

Look at John
lying in the woods.

The woodland creatures are gathering around him
laughing.

in little woodland voices.

MORAL: Even when you're looking up, don't forget to look down.

Ian McMillan

Practice questions

1 Find two things that relate to the time of day in both poems. *(1 mark)*

2 In the poem *Ten things …*, which lines might be in a poem that was *not* about magic? Give reasons for your answer. *(2 marks)*

3 Which one item in the list would you most like to have? Explain your reasons. *(3 marks)*

4 In the poem *Counting the stars*, what is John doing while he counts the stars? *(1 mark)*

5 Why do you think the poet wrote a moral at the end? *(2 marks)*

6 Which poem do you prefer? Explain the reasons for your choice. *(3 marks)*

See page 64 for the answers.

HOW DID YOU DO?

Handwriting

Handwriting is assessed in the Longer Writing Task, so do your best to keep it neat and easy to read. You can get a maximum of three marks for handwriting, and if you follow these hints and examples, they will be easy marks to achieve!

The golden rules

- Space out words and sentences evenly.
- Write on the lines if you are using lined paper.
- Use a pen or pencil you feel comfortable with and always use an eraser to rub out mistakes.
- Keep the letters the same size.
- Write so everyone can read your writing!

Example: 1-mark handwriting

If your handwriting looks like this, you need to work on:
- joining up letters so they flow together neatly
- keeping the letters the same size
- spacing out the letters evenly. Some of these words are quite squashed!

> Once upon a time. long ago there was a princess. She was the most beautiful princess in the world. Her dress sparkled as much as her charming atitude. She was the happiest prettiest person in the world.

Example: 2-mark handwriting

If your handwriting looks like this, you need to work on:
- making sure all, not just some, of the letters are joined together
- getting the ascenders (the upward strokes like *d* and *b*) to lean in the same direction.

> Once upon a time, long ago there was a princess. She was the most beautiful princess in all the land. Her dress Sparkled as much as her charming attitude. She was the happiest, prettiest person in the world.

Overall, the shape and size of the letters are even and the writing is easy to read.

Example: 3-mark handwriting

If your handwriting looks like this, you're going to get top marks! The letters are all correctly formed and are evenly sized and spaced. The other good thing about this handwriting is that it has its own style, so try to develop a style of your own.

> Once upon a time, long ago there was a princess. She was the most beautiful princess in all the land. Her dress sparkled as much as her charming attitude. She was the happiest, prettiest person in the world.

Hints and Tips	★ Compare a sample of your handwriting with the ones on this page. Which one is it most like? What are you doing well? What do you need to work on to make it better? ★ Go over what needs to improve with a highlighter pen, then rewrite the same sample, making as many improvements as you can. ★ Practise a few sentences at a time, rewriting them and making improvements. ★ Try especially hard to join the letters – it really speeds up writing!

Glossary

Adjectives words that add information or description to nouns

Adverbs words that add information or description to verbs

Cause what makes something happen

Character someone in a story; what someone is like, personality

Comprehension understanding

Conclusion the end of something; the resulting idea or thought about something

Connectives words that are used to link sentences and paragraphs

Deduction the use of evidence in the text to work out what the author is telling you, to read *between* the lines

Dialogue the words spoken by characters in a story

Effect the result of something happening

Emotive appealing to the emotions and making us feel in different ways

Evidence something that proves what you think or believe

Fiction stories that are imagined, not real

Imperative verbs that give a command, e.g. *Go* or *Put*

Inference the use of your own knowledge *and* the evidence in the text to come to a conclusion about what the author means, to read *beyond* the lines

Issue a matter or subject for discussion

Logical resulting naturally

Non-fiction texts that give you information

Omission missing out

Paragraphs a number of sentences grouped together, usually linked by idea, topic, time, place or theme

Passive voice a verb form where the action is done by someone else, e.g. *it was thrown*. The 'opposite' of this is the **active voice**, where the subject of the sentence does the action, e.g. *he threw it*

Possession owning

Problem something that goes wrong

Proper noun a noun that names a person, place or organisation

Recommendation what you think should be done

Resolution how a problem is sorted out

Review look back at critically or carefully

Setting where a story takes place

Stereotype a character, usually in a fairy story or traditional tale, who has no real distinguishing characteristics, e.g. *a bad witch, a handsome prince*

Summary a short piece of writing that sums up the main points

Theme an idea that a story or poem is about

Learning objectives for primary English

This chart shows you the objectives required to achieve Level 4 in English.

Strand	Year 5	Year 6
Word structure and spelling	• Spell words with unstressed vowels (*doctor*, *around*) • Know and use prefixes and suffixes like *im-*, *-ir-*, *-cian* • Group and classify words by their spelling patterns and their meanings	• Spell familiar words correctly; use a range of strategies to spell difficult or unfamiliar words • Edit, proofread and correct spelling in your own work, on paper and on screen
Understand and interpret texts	• Make notes on and use evidence from across a text • Infer writers' perspectives • Compare different types of texts; identify their structure • Know that a word can mean different things in different contexts • Explore how writers use language to create comic and dramatic effects	• Quickly decide on a text's value, quality or usefulness • Understand a text's themes, causes and points of view • Understand how writers use different structures to create an impact • Explore how word meanings change when used in different contexts • Recognise rhetorical devices used to persuade and mislead
Engage with and respond to texts	• Reflect on reading habits and plan your own reading goals • Know different ways to explore the meaning of texts • Compare how a theme is presented in poetry, prose and other media	• Read widely; discuss your own reading with others • Read longer texts • Compare how writers from different times and places present experiences and use language
Create and shape texts	• Reflect on your own writing; edit and improve it • Experiment with different forms and styles when writing stories, non-fiction and poetry • Use direct and reported speech, action and selection of detail to vary pace and viewpoint • Create multi-layered texts, including use of hyperlinks and linked web pages	• Set yourself challenges to extend achievement in writing • Use different techniques to engage and entertain the reader in narrative and non-narrative • Select words and language, drawing on your knowledge of literary features • Integrate words, images and sounds imaginatively for different purposes
Text structure and organisation	• Experiment with the order of sections and paragraphs to achieve different effects • Change the order of material within a paragraph, moving the topic sentence	• Use varied structures to shape and organise text coherently • Use paragraphs to achieve pace and emphasis
Sentence structure and punctuation	• Adapt sentence construction to different text types and readers • Punctuate sentences accurately, including using speech marks and apostrophes	• Express meanings, including hypothesis, speculation and supposition, by constructing sentences in varied ways • Use punctuation to clarify meaning in complex sentences
Presentation	• Adapt handwriting for specific purposes • Make informed choices about which ICT program to use for different purposes	• Use appropriate handwriting styles for different purposes • Select from a wide range of ICT programs to present text effectively and communicate information and ideas

Answers

Page 10 – Recount: Challenge

First, Next, Then, After, Finally

Page 11 – Recount: Example answer 1

Monday: Went to audition for school play. It's called The Lost Boys. We all went to the hall after school but not many boys came – Miss Jenkins was a bit cross. We'd to stand at the front one at a time and read a poem that Miss Jenkins gave to us. My voice shook! Aargh! But I got the part of the Nanny, though really wanted to be Wendy. Carly got Wendy. She's such a show-off. First rehearsal is lunch time tomorrow. I haven't got lots of lines to learn so that is good. Can't wait because I'm going to be a famous actor when I grow up!

Page 13 – Instructions and procedures:

Example answer 2

Getting dressed

What you need	What you do
Pants Socks T-shirt Trousers Sweatshirt Trainers	First put on the pants. These are small and white with three holes in them. Put your legs through the two smaller holes. Next put on the socks. There are two of these. They are long, grey tubes. Put one on each foot. Then put on the T-shirt. It goes over your head and has two holes for your arms. Put on the trousers. These are also grey but are much bigger than the socks. They go over the pants and socks. Now put on the sweatshirt over the T-shirt. It is blue and has a badge on the front. Finally put on the trainers. These are white and go on each foot. You will need to fasten the Velcro strips. Now you will look just like all the other pupils – apart from your green hair.

Page 14 – Non-chronological report:

Challenge

(Sample answer) Introduction, Appearance, Food, Habitat, Breeding

Page 15 – Non-chronological report:

Example answer 2

The Mintosaurus

Here you can see the newly discovered fossil of the Mintosaurus dinosaur.

This fossil was found by Sir Humbert Bumbert in South America in December 2008.

Amazing facts!

- *Length – 105 metres from nose to the tip of its tail.*
- *Height – 2 metres tall.*

- *Appearance – Mintosaurus had two short front legs and two powerful back legs. The front legs were short so it could bend down to graze. The back legs were strong to help it reach up to get leaves at the tops of trees. It had spines running down its back from the tip of its nose to the tip of its tail.*
- *Food – The Mintosaurus dinosaurs were herbivores. They ate the leaves of trees and also grazed on grass.*
- *Habitat – Mintosaurus has only been found in the jungles of South America.*
- *Did you know? The Mintosaurus dinosaur has been extinct for more than a million years!*

Page 17 – Explanation: Example answer 2

Dear Parents,

I am writing to tell you about a new type of lunch box that our class has invented. I hope it will make lunch times easier for your child.

The lunch box is made from recycled card, which means it is a greener box than the plastic ones most pupils use. It is split into four sections which open one after the other. This means your child will be able to eat the food in the right order. It also means that your child cannot just eat the bits they like!

There is one section for sandwiches. This opens first. When the sandwich section is empty, a spring goes off that opens the second section. This contains a drink. Next, the vegetable section opens. When the vegetable section is empty, the last section will open and your child can eat their fruit.

Using the new lunch box will help your child to eat a healthy meal at lunch time.

Yours sincerely,

Mr Andrews

Class 6A

Page 19 – Discussion: Example answer 2

Mobile phones should be allowed	Mobile phones should not be allowed
• Children can contact their friends • Parents can contact their children • Mobile phones are good fun • There are too many school rules already	• Children are already with their friends and don't need a phone to contact them • Parents can phone the school if they need to contact their children • They disrupt lessons • They cause jealousy about whose is the best phone

Page 20 – Persuasion: Challenge

have been offered, has been proven, should be eaten

Page 21 – Persuasion: Example answer 2

Football Stars Wanted!

Hill Street School Needs You!

Can you kick a football?

Can you run, tackle and dribble?

Do you want to learn how to play football?

Football is fun. You can make friends and keep fit too.

Hill Street School needs new players. Could you be one?
Try-outs
When – Thursday 12th September
Where – School playing field
Time – 3.30 p.m.
So Stop being a Couch Potato!
Come and be a Football Star!

Page 26 – Setting, characters and theme: Challenge 1

First extract: movement – strode; character – dangerous
Second extract: movement – stood straight and tall

Page 28 – Setting, characters and theme: Challenge 2

Lost and found

Beginning – Introduce one main character; establish setting
Build-up – Story gets going; character does something normal
Problem – Character finds or loses something or someone
Resolution – Lost thing/person is returned
Found thing/person not quite what it had seemed
Ending – Everything OK. Characters reflect on events

Wishing or wanting

Beginning – Introduce one main character; establish setting
Identify – What main character is wishing for or wanting
Build-up – Character goes in search of their wish
Problem – Character is stopped from getting what they want, often by another character
Resolution – Main character gets what he or she wanted
Ending – Character reflects on whether getting their wish was worth it

Page 29 – Dialogue: Challenge

1. surly, bad-tempered; **2.** angry;
3. very worried, concerned or afraid;
4. frightened or angry

Page 35 – Grammar: Challenge 4

Simple sentence – He didn't look back.
Compound sentence – Halfway into his voyage home, he could contain himself no longer and he opened the locket.
Complex sentence – He set sail into the night, delighted with his daring exploits and laughing with excitement at the thought of the riches he knew would be his.

Page 38 – Grammar: Challenge

1. The attack began well *although* they had been warned of our approach.
2. The waves continued crashing on the decks *until* everything below was soaked through.
3. He stopped running *because* his heart wasn't in it any more.

Page 41 Punctuation: Practice question

The ship had been becalmed before but never for so long. Some of the men lay about the decks that baked in the heat. Others stayed below hoping for cooler air, but the smell of so many men in a small space soon sent them on deck again. 'Was that a breath of wind?' asked the first mate hopefully.
'Perhaps it was,' said Cap'n Jake, 'I think you're right. All hand to the sails!' he cried, his voice reaching all through the tiny ship. Men, women and children went scurrying aloft.

Give yourself an extra mark if you remembered to start a new speaker on a new line!

Page 42 – Vocabulary: Challenge 1

(Sample answers)
1. This is an *EXCITING* story.
2. The train had *VIVID* purple doors.
3. After the race his face was *COMPLETELY SCARLET*.
4. Mrs Lane is *LIVID*.
5. The tree had *ENORMOUS* flowers on its branches.

Page 42 – Vocabulary: Challenge 2

dangerously, angrily

Page 43 – Vocabulary: Practice questions 1

(Sample answers)
1. He *suddenly* banged the book onto the table.
2. 'You look out!' he whispered *menacingly*.
3. The monkeys climbed *rapidly* from branch to branch.
4. 'It wasn't me!' she said *firmly*.

Page 43 – Vocabulary: Practice questions 2

(Sample answers)
1. Hordes of menacing monkeys *clambered* through the high treetops.
2. The proud princess *strode* along the streets of cheering crowds.
3. She *placed* the china cups carefully in the basket.
4. The thief *scrambled* through the broken attic window.

Page 44 – Spelling: Practice question

foxes, roads, bunches, wishes, sounds, lives, taxes, trees, drinks, pirates, houses, donkeys, flies, buses

Page 45 – Spelling: Challenge

Short vowel sound: bin, chat, flutter, wet, dot

Long vowel sound: line, paper, choose, reign, meet, light, float

Page 45 – Spelling: Quick challenge

Verb	Past tense	Present tense	Future tense
To fit	I fitted I have fitted I was fitting	I fit I am fitting	I will fit
To move	I moved I have moved I was moving	I move I am moving	I will move
To clap	I clapped I have clapped I was clapping	I clap I am clapping	I will clap
To keep	I kept I have kept I was keeping	I keep I am keeping	I will keep

continued over **63**

To swim	I swam I have swum I was swimming	I swim I am swimming	I will swim
To fly	I flew I have flown I was flying	I fly I am flying	I will fly
To produce	I produced I have produced I was producing	I produce I am producing	I will produce
To try	I tried I have tried I was trying	I try I am trying	I will try
To pursue	I pursued I have pursued I was pursuing	I pursue I am pursuing	I will pursue

Page 46 – Spelling: The spelling test

Section A

1. crunches   2. aunts   3. taxis
4. hippies   5. werewolves   6. lunches
7. ponies   8. chairs   9. sofas
10. hippopotami/hippopotamuses

Section B

'ing'
1. bat   batting
2. bale   baling
3. shoot   shooting
4. weep   weeping
5. slide   sliding

'ed'
1. snort   snorted
2. look   looked
3. map   mapped
4. glide   glided
5. shop   shopped

'er'
1. strong   stronger
2. loud   louder
3. big   bigger
4. white   whiter
5. bright   brighter

Section C

1. broke   2. grew
3. sharpened   4. skipped
5. stripes   6. actor
7. known   8. perfectly
9. thieves   10. reigned

Section D

dinosaurs, extinct, exactly, scientists, giant, dense, creatures, adapt, mammals, adaptable, species, successful, existed, threat, current

Page 51 – Reading comprehension:
Practice questions

1. 3 metres.
2. Dragons which live on Flores are red and yellow. Other Komodo dragons are greyish-brown.
3. Komodo, Rinca, Flores.
4. Carrion and live prey.
5. Reference to saliva, bacteria and blood poisoning.
6. Reference to specific actions compared to human wrestlers.
7. Carrion is the corpse of a dead animal. Live prey is living animals.
8. Ideas to combat hunting, loss of prey and habitat.

9. To influence the reader into wanting to conserve the dragons.
10. Scaly skin. Long tail. Long, forked yellow tongue.

Page 53 – Reading comprehension:
Practice questions

1. Cockpit.
2. The image of the burning plane.
3. A clump of thorn bushes.
4. Any three of the following phrases and sentences:
   His life went past in small, square pictures
   No time for developer and fixer
   No time for darkrooms and prints
   Too fast to focus upon
   As a cinema film rattles free of its spool, so Flash's fall rattled to an end
5. Any two phrases from the text.
6. He lost consciousness.
7. Can speak English, is practical, is a leader, intelligent, inquisitive, poor. (1 mark if only descriptions of her appearance are given.)

Page 55 – Reading comprehension:
Practice questions

1. The greenhouse effect.
2. Carbon dioxide, methane and water vapour.
3. The rainforests.
4. The melted ice would raise the sea levels.
5. *By the year 2050 the sea levels in Britain will have risen by up to half a metre.*
   150,000 people die each year as a direct result of climate change.
6. To make readers feel included and not being lectured to.
7. Answers will vary.
8. To make the reader answer them how the writer thinks they should and involve the reader.
9. Three marks if the answer refers to saving fossil fuels. Only one if it focuses solely on saving money.

Page 57 – Reading comprehension:
Practice questions

1. Cooper's Station.
2. Gum trees and wattle trees.
3. One day.
4. It was by sea. He says he was happy not to be sea-sick any more.
5. He was starting a new adventure.
6. No. The hymn repeating itself *remorselessly* in his head sounds as if it was a bad memory. He says he wasn't to know it then, but it heralded the *darkest* years of his life.

Page 58 – Reading comprehension:
Practice questions

1. A dark night. It's late at night.
2. A glass of water, full to the top. A large elephant. A snoring rabbit. They are all ordinary things and are only magical because they are in a wizard's pocket.
3. Answers will vary.
4. Walking through the woods and looking up at the sky.
5. Answers will vary.
6. Answers will vary.